THE BUTTERFLY GARDEN

THE BUTTERFLY GARDEN

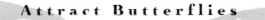

Creating Beautiful

Gardens to

Attract Butterflies

JERRY SEDENKO

Foreword by
Beth Callaway

Villard Books

NEW YORK 1991

A Running Heads Book

Copyright © 1991 by Running Heads Incorporated.

Library of Congress Cataloging-in-Publication Data

Sedenko, Jerry.
    Butterfly gardens : creating beautiful gardens
to attract butterflies / Jerry Sedenko. — 1st ed.
        p.   cm.
    Includes index.
    ISBN 0-394-58982-3
    1. Butterfly attracting.   2. Gardening to
attract wildlife.   3. Butterfly attracting — North
America.   4. Gardening to attract wildlife —
North America.   I. Title.
QL544.8.S43 1992
635.9′6 — dc20   91-50067
                                                      CIP

THE BUTTERFLY GARDEN
was conceived and produced by
Running Heads Incorporated
55 West 21 Street
New York, NY 10010

Editor: Charles de Kay
Designer: Jan Melchior
Managing Editor: Lindsey Crittenden
Production Manager: Linda Winters
Photo Editor: Ellie Watson
Photo Researcher: Tonia Smith

Illustrations by Linda Winters

Typeset by DIX Type
Color separations by Hong Kong Scanner Craft
    Company, Ltd.
Printed and bound in Singapore by Tien Wah Press
    (Pte.) Ltd.

9 8 7 6 5 4 3 2
First edition

**For Pop and Mother,
who gave me what I needed.**

ACKNOWLEDGMENTS

Thanks to Elvin McDonald, who paved the way.

*To Emily Bestler at Villard Books, for her
enthusiasm and support for this project.*

To Ann Lovejoy, for her encouragement.

*To Deb and Trish, for garden space and what little
computer knowledge I possess.*

To Susan Urstadt, for her thoroughness.

*To Flora and Fauna Books, Seattle, who, in
addition to being a remarkable
bookstore, conveniently provide seating
for browsers and researchers.*

To all my cohorts in the freemasonry of gardening.

To Mike, for being a pal.

CONTENTS

FOREWORD

Most of us have chased butterflies as children, admired their "wings of wonder" as adults, and pondered the whys and wherefores of their life cycle and place in the universe. Now we have this splendid book to guide us through the stages of inquiry. Jerry Sedenko presents the history, as well as the mystery, of these magnificent creatures — not to mention plant lists and plans for creating a butterfly garden.

Some of us may be so bold as to try our hand at butterfly gardening in our homes and gardens. Those gardeners with a warm sunroom, curiosity, and information have begun to enjoy a new dimension in gardening indoors. Many have also started with a few plants for butterflies in outdoor gardens or in city windowboxes. This book guides the butterfly gardener through the design of the garden and the choice of plants.

The love of natural beauty and a desire to create a fitting tribute to Cecil B. Day led Dean Day Smith to establishing a butterfly center in his name. The Cecil B. Day Butterfly Center at Callaway Gardens is a large conservatory where hundreds of species fly free as you walk through their favorite plants. The cupola that surmounts the roof of the butterfly center came from Virginia Hand Callaway's Victorian home. Upon cleaning the hardware before repainting, Callaway staff members were surprised to find engraved butterflies on the hinges and locks — testimony to the butterfly's tremendous popularity in the past.

Today, the butterfly is enjoying renewed popularity. At whatever level you enter the world of butterflies, pleasures and surprises certainly await you. Try it and enjoy!

Beth Callaway
Callaway Gardens
March 27, 1991

PREFACE

Northwestern Minnesota is by no means the ideal place for gardening. Winters of −40 degrees Fahrenheit followed by sweltering, muggy summers are a true test for plants. I dubbed my first garden "Easy Annuals"— Shirley poppies, nasturtiums, and, because my mother was from California, California poppies. In addition, she and I made forays into the woods for violets and columbines to augment the few delphiniums, bleeding hearts, hollyhocks, and the single hardy rose that managed to survive in our chicken-wire-enclosed flower garden. The bulk of our gardening efforts, of course, went toward more practical vegetable gardening. Our 1850s vintage farmhouse also had its quota of pink peonies and tawny daylilies, reminders of past owners, and a testament to the amazing durability of some plants. But the glory of the place was a thicket of lilacs, about seventy feet long. We picked armloads of lilac blossoms for the house and shared massive bouquets with neighbors.

My family and neighbors were not the only beneficiaries of this abundance, though. Dozens of butterflies flitted and flounced about the lilacs. Most vividly, I remember the Red Admirals, their dark wings flashing patches of brilliant scarlet. They were the first butterflies I really noticed. Soon after, I became aware of Monarchs and other milkweeds, tiny copper-tailed blues, and, dancing over the many fields of lavender-blue alfalfa blossoms, alfalfa butterflies.

My appreciation then was of the purest, most innocent sort, and it wasn't until we moved to California that I entered a darker period of butterfly study and began to collect them. There was a certain amount of challenge to chasing and netting the buckeyes, skippers, and California Sisters that I found in my new surroundings. But I always felt a twinge of guilt as I killed them with a quick dose of carbon tetrachloride. I didn't stick with collecting very long, although I did continue to frequent the big old butterfly bush that grew at the high school a block away, just to watch. And up the alley was the neighbors' passion vine, a rank tangle overwhelming the tumble-

A diminutive skipper, often found flitting about on lawns, takes time out to feed from the center of a cosmos, ABOVE. *An example of the flamboyant tropical species found in a butterfly house is this Malachite Butterfly,* OPPOSITE.

down fence that had once given it support. The vine's exotic ice-green and blue flowers and egg-shaped bright-orange fruit certainly made it the most decorative feature of the alley, but best of all were the dozen or so Gulf Fritillaries that could be found feasting there, their orange wings spangled with glinting silver.

Since then, I have seen butterflies in gentian-filled Alpine meadows, in the highlands of Scotland, and on Montana's flowery prairies. While on an orchid-hunting trip in Jamaica's Blue Mountains, I had butterflies follow me up to the edge of the cloud forest, where it became too cool for them to fly. And on Isla Mujeres, off the Caribbean coast of the Yucatán peninsula, hundreds of striped and vibrant butterflies flitted above a meadow surrounding ancient Mayan ruins.

It is easy to understand why the butterfly has come to symbolize the spirit; there is no more magical being. As these creatures silently dance through the air, gliding effortlessly from one flower to the next, they are the embodiment of all things ethereal. Though science tells us that they provide valuable pollination services and are just one more link in the food chain, we can't help but respond emotionally to butterflies. That such miraculous creatures exist at all is cause for wonder. But that they exist in such diversity, such extravagance of color, pattern, and shape, is a metaphor for the joys of life itself and reminds us that we are part of the miracle too.

ONE

MAGICAL CREATURES

If there is one creature on this planet that strikes the chord of fancy that dwells in all of us, surely it must be the butterfly. The ethereal nature and seemingly frivolous, elusive behavior of these insects speaks to our gentler, more romantic selves. Even scientists, departing from their usual no-nonsense approach, become sentimental when dealing with butterflies. Waxing poetic, they have given us brush-footed and gossamer-winged classes of butterflies, to name two. Common butterfly names show an even greater propensity for poetry. Some butterflies are named for their predominant color — the Silvery Blue, the Brown Elfin, sulphurs. Others get their names from the color patterns in their wings — dogfaces, crescentspots, and checkerspots. The "punctuation" tribe includes commas and the question mark. And then there's the butterfly royalty — the Monarch, the Queen, the Viceroy, and ladies (painted or otherwise) — with their military advisors — the Red Admiral and the White Admiral. One of the most evocative names aptly describes the garb of a large, dark-winged creature, the Mourning Cloak. The origin of the word "butterfly" is uncertain, but was probably first used to refer to butter-colored species.

For such creativity and affection to be lavished on any creature, particularly a lowly insect, is remarkable. Ah, but these are no ordinary creepy-crawlers. These are the apotheosis of all that is intriguing, fanciful, or beautiful in the six-legged world.

Before written history, in the time of legend, butterflies were often seen as a metaphor for the soul. The Nagas of Assam, India, believe that spirits of the dead undergo a series of changes in the Underworld, eventually returning to us as butterflies. Consequently, it is considered a disgrace to kill these insects. In Burma, the word for "soul" is the same as that for "butterfly." After the annual rice harvest, a trail of rice hulls leads from the fields to the granary, to help guide the rice's soul to safety.

An old Serbian belief holds that the soul of a sleeping witch leaves her body as a butterfly. If the witch is turned end-for-end, the returning butterfly will not find the witch's mouth again, and she will die!

On a more positive note, Samoans were of the opinion that butterflies were manifestations of the gods and must never be harmed. And among certain Brazilian Indians, the dead are honored by a pair of masked dancers who assume the attitude of the iridescent-blue *Morpho* butterfly by fluttering about before settling down.

One of the most charming legends is the Papago Indian story of how butterflies were created. In the autumn of the year, the Great Spirit grew wistful at

Size and color differences between the sexes are exhibited by these two tropical Dryas julia butterflies, seen here in mating position, RIGHT.

the idea of the bounty of summer being soon laid waste by winter. So he took flecks of color from the autumn leaves, white from cornmeal, and blue from the summer sky. These he placed in a leather bag and gave the pouch to some children, who, of course, could not resist examining the magic parcel's contents. Much to everyone's delight, out flew hundreds of butterflies, their wings covered with the bits of color.

Images of the butterfly are a recur-ring motif in the art of antiquity. Egyptian frescoes at Thebes and ancient Chinese and Japanese decorative objects were adorned with butterflies. Early Greeks used butterfly imagery to represent the human soul and ornamented their pottery with winged creatures that were half human and half butterfly. It was an easy thing for the first Christians, many of whom were Greek, to transfer this symbolism to the Resurrection. Consequently, dur-

ing the years of Roman persecution, the butterfly, along with the fish and other ideograms, became a visual "password" among the faithful.

The butterfly has also qualified as an artistic subject in its own right, without symbolic overtones. Still-lifes by the great Flemish painters depicted butterflies and other insects. These artists' painstaking efforts have left such accurate images that the species represented are easily identifiable.

Butterflies also frequent the literary world. In the fourth century B.C., the Chinese scribe, Chuang-Tzu, penned, "I do not know whether I was then a man dreaming I was a butterfly, or whether I am now a butterfly dreaming I am a man."

More than two millennia later, the butterfly was still a potent literary topic. Thomas Hood, the mid-Victorian English poet, used the butterfly as a symbol for the bounty of summer in his poem *No!*:

No warmth, no cheerfulness,
*   no healthful ease,*
no comfortable feel in any member —
no shade, no shine, no butterflies, no bees,
no fruits, no flowers, no leaves, no birds,
November.

It's quite possible that this association of butterflies with summer led to the labeling of British cab drivers who worked only during the fair season as "butterflies."

Another writer of the same era, Lewis Carroll, wrote in *Through the Looking Glass* of

butterflies that sleep among the wheat.
I make them into mutton-pies,
And sell them in the street.

By contrast, Charles Dickens portrayed butterflies not as helpless victims but as symbols of independence.

A female Black Swallowtail, OPPOSITE, *spreads her wings broadly to absorb the heat of the morning sun. A Tiger Swallowtail,* ABOVE, *feeds on a zinnia blossom.*

In *Bleak House,* he declared, "I only ask to be free. The butterflies are free. Mankind will surely not deny to Harold Skimpole what it concedes to the butterflies!"

Twentieth-century writers have also turned to the butterfly to enliven their prose and poetry. The American mas-

The profuse, sunny flowers of hybrid coreopsis entice many a butterfly, ABOVE.

ter of hard-boiled detective fiction, Raymond Chandler, features a butterfly in setting a mood of stultifying heat: "A large black and gold butterfly fishtailed in and landed on a hydrangea bush almost at my elbow, moved its wings slowly up and down a few times,

then took off heavily and staggered away through the motionless hot scented air."

Russian-born author Vladimir Nabokov, an eloquent butterfly observer and enthusiast, describes his memories of the family *dacha* and the butterflies of his childhood in *Speak, Memory.* He is credited with discovering twelve new species and subspecies, including the Nabokov's Pug. His poem *A Discovery* expresses the author's literary and scientific interests, recounting his feelings upon finding one of these new species. He relates where and when he found it, why it qualifies as a new species, and its value as a bit of scientific information. Yet it is the simple existence of the tiny creature that is its most important quality:

*Dark pictures, thrones, the stones that
 pilgrims kiss,
poems that take a thousand years to die
but ape the immortality of this
red label on a little butterfly.*

Nabokov was not the first philosophical type to explore the butterfly. The scientific study of butterflies begins with Aristotle, who first described the life cycle of the cabbage butterfly. His observations were sounder than those of Albertus Magnus, who, in his thirteenth-century *De Natura Animalum,* called butterflies "flying worms."

The seventeenth century saw the awakening of curiosity about the realm of Nature. The wealthy maintained "cabinets of curiosities," full of bones, fossils, shells, stuffed animals, and insects. John Evelyn, diarist and roving emissary for James I of England, visited the "private museum" of a Signor Septalla in Milan, and was shown "much amber full of insects." In 1644, Evelyn visited M. Morine in Paris and observed, "His collection of all sorts of insects, especially of butterflies, is most curious: he keeps them in drawers, so placed as to represent a beautiful piece of tapestry. . . ."

Initially, there was no particular organization to these collections of biological curios, but as the Age of Exploration continued, the wealth of new and unusual natural objects being brought home to Europe prompted several scientists to attempt to bring some order to it all.

Foremost among these was the Swedish naturalist Carl von Linné, better known to us by his Latinized name, Carolus Linnaeus. In the 1700s, he developed the binomial (two-word) system of nomenclature that we still use today. The first word of the scientific name is the genus, which refers to a group of closely related organisms. The second word indicates an individual species. Originally, Linnaeus placed all butterflies in the genus *Papilio*. Little did he realize how many changes and reclassifications would occur in the years since. For his efforts, he was honored by the Swedish royal family, whose Queen Lorisa Ulrika became a close friend and fellow butterfly collector.

At this same time, in England, a journal of the exploits of butterfly collectors came into being. The first issue of *The Aurelian*, in 1766, had illustrations that were truly works of art. The issue's frontispiece shows two gentlemen pursuing butterflies in a woodland glade. They are using the clumsy and curious "bat folder" or "clap net" devices of the day. Consisting of a three-foot *U*-shaped frame, hinged in the middle and covered with netting, these contraptions required the use of both hands, and a lot of agility.

Butterfly collectors were not given the respect that today's scientists are. Indeed, they were regarded with curiosity and some disdain. The story is told of a Lady Glanville, for example, whose will was contested after her death on grounds of insanity. It was deemed that "none but those who were deprived of their senses would go in pursuit of butterflies."

In the 1800s, the century of the Great Collectors, butterfly collecting materials and methods, as well as regard for its enthusiasts, improved substantially. Some notable people exhibited a fascination with butterflies. A pair of intrepid ladies poked about Europe, indulging the Victorian mania for collecting. Mary de la Beche resided in Wales, but combed the hinterlands of some of the less-traveled areas of eastern and western Europe. Englishwoman Margaret Fountaine retold her exploits in books with the intriguing titles of *Butterflies and Late Love* and *Love Among the Butterflies.* While in Hungary with members of the Budapest Entomological Society in 1898, Fountaine wrote, ". . . after more than two hours of bumping and jolting along we arrived — an entomologist's dream realized, a forest abounding with butterflies. . . ." She enjoyed the company immensely, saying she had "never met a nicer set of men" than these fellow scientists.

A bit later, in the early 1900s, Walter and Charles Rothschild employed as many as ten people to search the globe for their respective private collections. Charles Rothschild is said to have pulled the emergency cord to stop a train so that he could pursue a rare butterfly he had glimpsed.

What's all the fascination about? How could such seemingly insignificant little creatures have prompted proper Victorian ladies and gentlemen to forsake their drawing rooms and don pith helmets? And why today do butterflies continue to capture our appreciation and emotions?

First, since some confusion often exists, let us distinguish between butterflies and moths. Butterflies have knobs on the ends of their antennae, whereas moths have feathered antennae, typically tapering to a point. Butterfly bodies are slender; moth bodies commonly are thick and very fuzzy. Butterflies hold their wings upright when at rest, while moths hold theirs horizontally. All butterflies fly during the day but most moths prefer the darker hours. Finally, butterflies, except for the skippers, have naked, parchmentlike pupal cases; moths spin fiber strands (silk) into cocoons.

Unique in the insect world, butterflies are distinguished by a variety of truly remarkable traits. They are sensitive to a broader range of light wavelengths than is any other creature, able to see both the full spectrum visible to us and ultraviolet light. Many flowers have evolved "nectar guides," concentric bands or rays of contrasting color that help a butterfly zero in on a nectar source. Frequently, these are visible only in ultraviolet light, and what appears to us as an unassuming monochromatic flower may display patterns that shout "Eat here!" to a butterfly.

Butterflies also exhibit some unusual behavioral traits. To the untrained eye, one butterfly in flight seems very like another. But the frenetic darting of skippers, the stately gliding of swallowtails, the graceful motion of Mourning Cloaks are all flight patterns highly characteristic of each species. And in the throes of butterfly love, mating butterflies demonstrate dashing dips, paired upward spiraling, and other extravagant flight behavior.

Some males display a "patroling flight pattern" that apparently hints at a territorial streak in their nature. Many times a male acts as sentry, flying up and down a certain space which he has chosen as his own, usually the borderlands between woodland and meadow. The males of other species guard vantage points, such as hilltops or treetops, driving out any other male who blunders into their territory. Forest clearings, where rays of sunlight show off a butterfly's brilliance to a stunning advantage, are often jealously guarded. Intruders are driven off amid violent, but usually harmless, flutterings. Interestingly enough, interlopers are nearly always defeated, with the original occupant retaining not only the territory but also the exclusive mating rights that go with it.

Another behavior pattern that only the males exhibit has been termed "puddling." Butterflies can frequently be seen grouped around the edges of water puddles. Early observers assumed that the butterflies were simply drinking the water. Later, it was noticed that the butterflies engaging in this behavior were exclusively males. Further investigation revealed that it was connected with mating. When a male fertilizes a female, he includes a "package" of sodium salts that help keep her healthy and productive of viable eggs. This depletes his sodium reserves, and, to replenish them, he gathers with other breeding males at what are essentially mineral-rich butterfly salt-licks. If the salts are dilute, the butterflies are required to pump a great deal of liquid through their systems in order to concentrate enough sodium for their requirements. At these times, droplets of water can be seen emerging from the end of each butterfly's abdomen.

On stones bordering these puddling sites, butterflies will be seen engaging in another common ritual. Though they appear to be simply resting in a sunny spot, in actuality they are absorbing heat from the sun. Butterflies are unable to fly if they're too cold. Because they're "cold-blooded" creatures, they can't generate their own heat. As they slowly flex their wings, they absorb the sun's energy in the form of flight-enabling heat. Some butterflies spend up to 80 percent of the day in this basking behavior. Tropical butterflies, inhabiting the warmer areas of the globe, have few worries on this score. But dwellers of the arctic and mountainous regions have evolved two methods for greater heat-absorption

efficiency. Some have developed dark coloration, which is logical, since dark colors absorb more heat than do light colors. But many butterflies in these regions are pale-colored and even white. What could be the adaptive advantage of this? A close look at these butterflies reveals that they have dark

bodies and wing bases. In addition, instead of holding their wings vertically when resting, these butterflies keep them partially spread, in a *V* shape. The method behind this madness is heat reflection. True, the pale wing color reflects heat, but in this case, it is reflected toward the dark body and wing bases. Since this is where the flight muscles are, the heat goes directly to where it is most useful.

As denizens of the daylight, all butterflies seek out protected spots to spend the night. Most find the underside of a leaf in a dense thicket or tree to be to their liking. At twilight, if you watch closely, you can see butterflies searching for roosting places. They flit and hover near shrubs, obviously looking for something. When they choose a spot, they seem to vanish before your very eyes! This is partly a result of the deepening darkness, and partly a result of the butterflies' coloration. Even the most brightly colored butterflies have dull underwings. With their wings folded for the night, they easily blend into their surroundings. So your eye, accustomed to following flashes of scarlet or gold, is fooled into thinking that the butterfly has simply disappeared. If this trick works on you, you can assume that it works equally well on any hungry bird.

Most butterflies roost individually,

It's easy to see how the "false eyes," on this butterfly, OPPOSITE, *could confuse a predator. The dark veins and body of the Clodius Parnassian butterfly,* ABOVE, *concentrate heat absorption where it's needed most.*

the logic being that singly they are more difficult to detect. Others roost communally, however, in groups of up to a few dozen. The advantage of this "safety in numbers" is similar to that enjoyed by schools of fish, flocks of birds, or herds of antelope. A predator becomes overwhelmed by the sheer numbers of prey, and by the confusion that results when so many individuals take flight. Not knowing where to strike, the attacker often finds that its quarry escapes unscathed.

Since butterflies need the morning sun to "get their engines running," they frequently orient themselves on their roost to take advantage of the sunrise. Even if they have come to rest on the western side of the roost, many butterflies make their way during the night to an eastern exposure.

All of these fascinating behaviors have evolved over millions of years, unseen or unheeded by humans until relatively recently, when those observant Victorians took to the woods and fields. And it's only within the last few years that the idea of luring the butterflies to *us* has begun to catch on. This has happened for a number of reasons. First, the collectors and amateur naturalists of the eighteenth and nineteenth centuries had a huge expanse of untouched natural environment to explore, which is no longer our lot

today. The natural world has shrunk to a fraction of its former size. True, some butterflies, such as the cabbages and alfalfas, have adapted very well to sharing their environment with humans. But many species find their world disappearing. Already one species on the San Francisco peninsula has become extinct, and there are approximately ten others listed as endangered in the United States.

In the past, as humanity strove to dominate the natural world, untold damage was done. We now realize that it is within our power to end, and even reverse, the damage. Creating a garden that welcomes butterflies is one small way that we can help right the situation. When we plant our gardens in such a way as to make them spiritually and aesthetically pleasing to ourselves, it is also possible to make a place for butterflies and other wild creatures. We reap the double benefit of not only being able to enjoy a beautiful garden, but also of deriving satisfaction from knowing that we are making room for other dwellers of our planet.

Perhaps you're a bit concerned that all your efforts at plant nurturing will be laid to waste by armies of munching caterpillars. Not to worry. The larvae of many butterflies prefer to feed on "undesirables," if not downright weeds. Painted Ladies eat thistles,

Monarchs eat milkweed, and a host of butterflies love nettles. At last you have an excuse for being a little bit lazy and allowing these nuisance plants to exist on the fringes of your garden — you can simply say that you left them for the butterflies! But even the caterpillars that feed on your choicer garden beauties are beset by such a large number of predators and parasites that the risk of losing a plant to their attentions is very small. If you find that your favorite plant is also a favorite with your butterflies, grow more of it so that there will be enough for everybody!

Just which butterflies can you expect to lure into your floral world? That depends on what part of the country you live in. The native butterfly that you are likely to attract can be found in any good field guide, or you might contact some of the butterfly advocacy groups listed in the Appendices. While it may be true, for instance, that the Giant Swallowtail feeds on citrus trees, if you live in Minneapolis and put your Meyer lemon outdoors for the summer, don't expect Giant Swallowtails to flock to your garden. If a butterfly doesn't occur naturally in your region, there's little point in tailoring your garden to meets its needs.

By the same token, it's just possible that you live in an area that has a high percentage of rare or exceptional butterfly species. Catering to their needs can bring the extra reward of helping to preserve a unique creature whose very existence is in jeopardy.

Even if none of the rarer butterflies deign to bestow their presence on your garden, the joy you will take from hosting even the most common of species will repay you for your efforts.

Eastern Tiger Swallowtail, ABOVE.

~

TWO

THE
LIFE
CYCLE

As wondrous as the butterfly itself

is, the sequence of events that leads

from minute egg to winged adult is

truly astonishing. All butterflies go

through the same four develop-

mental stages: egg, larva (caterpil-

lar), pupa, and adult. Each of these

incarnations is so remarkably different that it's difficult to believe you're looking at the same creature, and not four completely different ones. And yet, the entire process takes just a few weeks, some of which are actually spent in the adult stage.

One of the most familiar of North American butterflies—with a range that covers most of the United States, except for the Northwest—is the Monarch (*Danaus plexippus*), and its bold black and orange tiger-striped wings also make it one of the most easily distinguished. The Monarch has perhaps the most fascinating life cycle of any of our native butterflies, and serves as a good example of the developmental changes that occur in all butterflies.

Within hours of mating, a female butterfly seeks out the proper host plant for the future caterpillars to eat. In the Monarch's case, host plants are always types of milkweed (*Asclepias* spp.). Many other species of butterflies are just as careful in their choice of where to lay their eggs. The Giant Swallowtail prefers citrus trees, while the Pipevine and Spicebush Swallow-

The dark spot in the center of each lower wing identifies this Monarch, ABOVE, *as a male.*

tails choose the plants from which they take their name. Gulf Fritillary eggs and larvae are found on passion vines; the whites on members of the mustard family; and the sulphurs on clovers. Such host-specific butterflies rely on plants that have a rather wide range. Other butterflies are generalists, and at any given time of the breeding season favor the most succulent local plants.

Back at the milkweed patch, the female Monarch hovers, using her senses of smell and taste to determine just which plants are milkweeds. Alighting on the underside of a leaf, she curls her abdomen down and under, between her legs, and deposits a single egg. She will do this as many as 700 times in the same number of different locations. There is a greater chance of a single tiny egg going undetected by predators and hatching than there is of a more highly attractive massing of eggs surviving. Also, on the underside of the leaf, the egg is protected from the elements.

Shaped like a fancifully ridged and faceted hen's egg, a butterfly egg is less than 2mm by 1.2mm, about the size of the head of a pin, and weighs a mere half milligram. Initially creamy yellow, it changes to dark gray in three to four days, with a dark spot that will eventually become the caterpillar's head. Although the eggs of some butterfly

A Giant Swallowtail, North America's largest butterfly, displays its bold patterns, ABOVE. *The intricately structured, exotic passionflower,* BELOW, *is a beloved food of the Gulf Fritillary.*

species are adapted to withstanding the rigors of winter, most butterfly eggs hatch in the summer within two weeks of being laid. In the case of the Monarch, temperatures in the eighties promote rapid development, and soon the tiny being wriggles out of its shell. Once this is accomplished, the newly emerged larva consumes its eggshell. From then on, a steady (and I do mean steady) diet of tender young milkweed leaves is all the caterpillar will eat. This nonstop gorging goes on for fifteen days, until the larva grows to two inches. By comparison, if a six-pound human baby grew at the same rate, in two weeks it would weigh eight tons!

All insects have external skeletons made of a material called chitin, even a soft-bodied caterpillar. Unfortunately, chitin does not expand and grow along with the larva, so the "skin" must be shed, or molted, as the caterpillar increases in size. Before each molt, the caterpillar quits eating and remains motionless for up to a day. The exoskeleton loses its flexibility and splits down the back, revealing the preformed exoskeleton of the next stage, or instar. The caterpillar wriggles its way out of the old "skin," leaving the shriveled husk behind as it commences eating, and growing, again. This happens four times in the case of the Monarch. Each time, the striped pattern

One at a time, the female Monarch deposits her hundreds of eggs on the undersides of milkweed leaves, BELOW.

Emerging from its egg, this tiny first instar caterpillar begins its nonstop eating, ABOVE.

The gaudy fifth (and final) instar, BELOW, *has the discarded skin of the fourth at its feet.*

The final molt of the Monarch carterpillar produces this celadon-and-gold pupa, ABOVE.

intensifies in color, so that the last stage finds the caterpillar with a bold array of cream, black, and orange latitudinal stripes. One would think that such a striking pattern would make the caterpillar too noticeable to predators, but for some reason, not many find the Monarch larva appealing. One theory is that eating bitter milkweed makes the caterpillar unappetizing. Other species bristle with colored spines or hornlike structures. Some are highlighted with brilliant spots or large false "eyes" on their less-vulnerable rear end that decoy a predator away from the true head.

Even though the caterpillar resembles a worm, it has the three insect body regions of head, thorax, and abdomen. The head's main feature is a prodigious pair of jaws, well suited to shearing off and ingesting leaf tissue. The thorax has three segments, each with a pair of true legs, ending in clawed feet. The abdomen bears five pairs of bristly "false" legs, or "prolegs." At its rear, separated by a gap, are a pair of anal prolegs, used in forming the pupal stage. Despite all those legs and gripping claws, occasionally a caterpillar will fall to the ground. Should this happen, the caterpillar instinctively remains motionless for a time, "playing possum" so as to appear dead and uninteresting to a potential predator. Other species' methods of protection include feeding on undersides of leaves, feeding at night, and camouflage coloring. Some even spray chemicals to discourage predators.

When a caterpillar has reached maturity, it crawls away from its milkweed patch in search of a quiet, pro-

Fully formed, the adult Monarch can be seen through its now-transparent case, ABOVE.

tected spot, one that will offer support for the pupa and shelter from the sun and rain. The caterpillar goes through a period of lethargy, then gets down to the business of forming the pupa.

First, the caterpillar spins a small web of silk and deposits it on the chosen supporting structure. A raised "button" of silk, about 3mm high, is formed in the center. The caterpillar grips this with its anal prolegs while it hangs, upside-down, in a *J* shape. Soon, the body relaxes and hangs limply, while the final split in the exoskeleton begins. A new form, the pupa, squirms and contorts violently in order to shed the final vestiges of its former self. If this old "skin" weren't completely shaken off, it could tighten and interfere with the development of the adult butterfly. Simultaneously, a special barbed hooklike structure on the upper end of the pupa, the cremaster, is inserted into the silk button. Secure attachment is crucial, as a fall of even an inch at this critical time would mean death or permanent disfigurement to the fragile pupa. A well-chosen site, protected from rain, becomes particularly important now, as the supporting silk button will dissolve in water and the pupa could fall.

After a few hours, the pupal casing hardens into a parchment cask, bejeweled with golden dots. These brilliant flecks are more than ornmamental. Experiments have shown that each dot is in some way responsible for pigment formation in various regions of the wings of the adult Monarch butterfly.

Two weeks later, the black and

orange stripes of the wings can be seen through the now-transparent pupal case. Somehow the pupa is able to sense weather conditions, since an adult rarely emerges during stormy periods. When emergence, or meta-morphosis, does occur, it happens quickly, and usually in the morning, so as to take advantage of a whole day's worth of warmth and vivifying sun-light. The pupal case splits and the adult, with its crumpled and shriveled wings, crawls out in just over a minute. It remains clinging to the pupal case for two to seventeen hours. During this time, it pumps a clear greenish fluid from its body into its wings. Initially, the body is swollen out of proportion, but as fluid is pumped from it to the wings, a more familiar shape appears. The wings fill out and straighten, tak-ing on the characteristics that are the crowning glory of the adult Monarch butterfly. The wings flex, slowly at first, testing their strength. And then, suddenly, the butterfly is airborne, leaving behind all memory of its former earthbound existence.

Butterfly wings are a marvel of color and function. The actual wings are composed of a transparent membrane, stretched between a strengthening web of veins. Covering this membrane are thousands of minute scales. The Greek word for scale is *lepis*, and it is from

this that the large order of butterflies takes its name, Lepidoptera, meaning "scaly-winged."

Scales are not only on a butterfly's wings. They cover virtually its entire body surface, in different sizes and densities. But it is the wing scales that produce the most striking color effects.

The adult Monarch emerges and begins pumping fluids into its wings, ABOVE.

Some of these scales are filled with pig-ment, such as brown, black, orange, yellow, red, and white, and, when grouped together on the wing mem-brane, produce areas of these colors. Another type of scale is responsible for the gaudy displays of purple and violet, blue, silver, and green; for the flashes of silver; and for metallic sheen. These scales have tiny parallel ridges that act as microscopic prisms, refracting light into rainbow hues. The same effect is produced by certain feathers on birds, such as the ones on the throat patches of hummingbirds. Depending on the angle of the light striking them, these prismatic areas will either be dark and dull, or flash with dazzling brilliance. Each scale is a particle of pure color, and when these elements are arranged in patterns, much like a pointillist painting, the resulting color pattern is produced. No doubt you have at some time caught a butterfly and managed to rub off some of these scales. They appear as dust on your fingers, and leave behind a smudged or transparent area on the creature's wings. No need to worry if the butterfly can still fly; scales don't affect flight. But without the color patterning proper to its species, the butterfly may not find a mate who will recognize it. A butterfly's wings are not merely an ornamental mode of locomotion. Their color and pattern help members of the species to recognize each other, as well as act as camouflage from predators.

The differences between most species can be seen in their different wing patterns. But to the human eye, the

The female counterpart of the boldly striped male

Tiger Swallowtail is dusky in color, ABOVE.

differences between male and female are generally much less obvious. True, some butterfly species, notably the swallowtails, often show pronounced sexual differences. Males are often boldly striped, whereas females might be a glossy blue-black. But even sexes that appear identical to our eyes may possess subtle but marked differences when seen from the butterflies' viewpoint, with their ability to see both the full spectrum and ultraviolet light.

The wings of many butterflies, and most moths, help to conceal them from attackers. Some species exhibit cryptic coloration, which makes their wings resemble the color and texture of a particular kind of branch or leaf they frequent. Others show disruptive coloration, which means that the outline of the butterfly is "disrupted" by irregular patterning, confusing the predator so that it will not recognize the butterfly for the tasty morsel it really is. A third defensive method is mimicry: the butterfly resembles something else, generally of a distasteful or frightening nature. The tropics-dwelling owl butterfly has large wing spots that look like owl eyes, and the shape of its body echoes that of an owls' beak! The owl butterfly is most active near dusk, when real owls are abroad, completing the masquerade. Other butterflies carry the deception to less of an extreme, and simply try to fool a hungry bird into going for a seemingly vulnerable "eye," which, in reality, is merely a spot on the butterfly's wing. More often than not, while the wing may be torn, the butterfly escapes.

The "tails" of swallowtail butterflies may seem to be flashy extravagances, with no protective value. But remember that a butterfly rests with its wings held vertically. In outline, the "tails" look like a very prominent head, and the attacker aims for the "wrong" end.

The caterpillars of several species also display mimicry of a somewhat comical nature. Particularly in the first instars (the caterpillar's first set of "skin"), they have patterns of gray and white that make them look for all the world like bird droppings.!

The value of all these features that fool predators is obvious. But what of patterns and colors that border on the garish? Of what possible protection could they be?

Most of the lurid-winged species possess, like the Monarch, an ability to concentrate and store toxins in their bodies, rendering them at the very least distasteful, and, in certain cases, downright poisonous. These noxious compounds aren't actually manufactured by the butterfly. Rather, the caterpillar feeds on plants containing them, and concentrates the substances in its body,

with no apparent harm to itself. Often, such caterpillars are themselves brazenly colored and festooned with all manner of showy bristles. They're stating in no uncertain terms that they aren't to be confused with any other, more tasty species — the insect version of "You'll be sorry!" Cabbage butterflies are so inedible because they concentrate mustard oil glycosides in their bodies from the Brassica family, whose plants comprise their larval food source. To most animals, these are highly toxic compounds. But not to humans. So we inadvertently help these species by planting cabbages, Brussels sprouts, and broccoli by the acre. The butterflies' ubiquitous creamy-white wings flag a sharp warning to any bird with dinner on its mind.

After the wings, the next most obvious feature of an adult butterfly is its antennae, tipped with a knoblike structure. When viewed under a microscope, the spongy, pitted surface is apparent. These convolutions allow for a maximum absorption of scent, which is the primary function of the antennae. But the antennae also act as gravitational sensors, allowing a butterfly to know which way is "up." During the seemingly chaotic flutterings, such knowledge comes in handy, indeed.

One of the structures that make a butterfly unique is its proboscis. This acts much as a hollow soda straw to suck nectar and fruit juices, but it is not a single hollow tube. Instead, the jaws, or maxilla, found on other insects have on the butterfly become greatly elongated and convex. They fit together, much like the halves of a zipper, to form a hollow tube that can be coiled when not in use, or extended to probe for liquid nourishment.

The jointed legs and feet of butterflies serve as more than support for when a butterfly lands. They also have taste sensors. When a butterfly wades in fruit juice, the reaction is to extend its proboscis in a feeding gesture, but when the liquid is water, no such response is elicited. Also, when a female is about to deposit her eggs, she will flutter near what she senses is the "right" plant. By grazing a leaf with her feet she can "taste" it to make sure.

Butterfly eyes are typical insect eyes, composed of hundreds of individual facets, called ommatidia, which each produces an image. The way these facets are grouped, with up to 6,000 ommatidia in each bulging compound eye, ensures 360-degree vision, so that nothing escapes detection. Precise detail is impossible, but the mosaic of vision produced gives a butterfly a good sense of its immediate surroundings. The butterfly's ability to see ultraviolet light is beneficial at feeding time,

as will be seen later. In addition, a butterfly is also able to sense polarized light, which enables it to orient itself in relation to the sun's position, and aids in navigation.

The primary function of an adult butterfly is to reproduce. If you're fortunate enough to spot a male and female engaging in their pre-nuptial flight, keep watching. What follows is fascinating.

First, it will be helpful to distinguish between the sexes. In the Monarch, our chosen example, they resemble one another closely. However, the male Monarch has heavier dark lines on his wings, and in the center of each lower wing there is a dark dot, the alar spot. This is a scent gland, used to attract the female and to keep her interest from flagging during mating. Also, where there are stands of milkweed plants, upon which they will lay their eggs, you are likely to find a preponderance of females waiting for males. Conversely, for reasons that are open to speculation, greater concentrations of males are to be found where nectar-bearing flowers bloom in abundance.

A breeding male will fly to an area near a concentration of milkweed and stake out a small territory. Should a female enter his area, the male will follow. If she is receptive to his advances, the female ascends in a spiral, pursued by her suitor. Together, they fly to a nearby branch and get down to serious business.

The male's anal gland, a feathery plume, secretes a flowery aroma that the female finds irresistible. She responds by uncoiling her proboscis as if to feed. The male then struts up beside her, head next to head, and bends his abdomen laterally to contact hers. Structures called abdominal claspers hold the female firmly while his sperm are deposited in her abdominal cavity. Here, she holds them until they are needed, passing them down the oviduct to fertilize her eggs. When this happens, she seeks out the underside of a milkweed leaf, and the life cycle repeats itself.

A reproductively mature female Monarch lives for thirty to forty days, sipping nectar and depositing eggs. A male lives for twenty to seventy days if it reproduces in summer (these figures are somewhat speculative, however, as vastly differing life expectancies have been reported by scientific observers). The adults of other species live for varying lengths of time, some as little as three days. Since the main purpose of all adult butterflies is to reproduce, once that has been accomplished, they die. The reproductive period can occur any time during mid- to late summer. In the case of the Monarch, however,

in late summer a generation of nonreproductive adults emerges to embark on a most remarkable journey, incidentally becoming the longest-lived of all butterflies, surviving up to ten months.

In the case of several species of North American butterflies, the overwintering stage is the pupa. Not so with the Monarch. In August and September, this brood of wanderers begins to aim its flight in a southerly direction. There are two paths of migration, one for Monarchs from west of the Rockies, and the other used by the much larger eastern population. From as far north as Ontario, this latter group trends toward the Gulf of Mexico, convening in large flocks over the eastern seaboard. Mile after mile they make their way toward their wintering quarters, flying quite close to the ground in order to take advantage of nectar. The migrants never change their direction, and will fly over an obstacle rather than go around it.

Like all butterflies, Monarchs roost at night. Because they are cold-blooded, they must find each roosting site while the air temperature is still above 50 degrees Fahrenheit or they enter a state of semi-paralyzed torpor. If caught out in the open, they become easy prey. In the morning, the sun warms the air so the butterflies can move again, and once more they're off.

In their millions, they cross the Gulf, continuing their journey to they know not where. And that is part of the miracle. Since the members of this migratory generation will live only long enough to make the journey once, they are obviously *not* exhibiting learned behavior. What, then, causes these

A colorful close relative of the Monarch, the Queen, ABOVE, *is just as unpalatable to predators.*

mere wind-tossed scraps of life to embark on a journey of thousands of miles? And what is the guiding principle that directs them to a few certain trees in a remote region of central Mexico? It remains a mystery.

On they fly, until, in November, they reach their destination 9,000 feet south of Mexico City. There, they come to rest in just a few groves of tall, gray-green *oyamel* trees (a kind of fir), blanketing the trees so heavily that boughs sometimes break under their massed weight. Since a hundred Monarchs weigh scarcely an ounce, you begin to sense just how many there are.

The climatic conditions in these mountains are ideal for overwintering. The temperature hovers just above the freezing point, so the butterflies remain nearly motionless. In this state of suspended animation, the Monarchs burn little of the fat reserves needed to make the return trip northward.

The same conditions exist in certain areas along the central California coast, where the western population overwinters. There, the Monarchs' regular appearance is cause for the annual Butterfly Festival in Pacific Grove, culminated by the crowning of the Butterfly Queen.

City law there forbids the molestation of the Monarchs, but such is not the case in Mexico. A movement is under way to protect the butterfly groves, but as yet the trees, which are on privately held land, are vulnerable to felling by woodcutters.

In late January, the days begin to lengthen and the air begins to warm.

Bright "false eyes" stand out on the otherwise dull wings of this Grayling.

In the *oyamel* groves, the Monarchs begin to increase their movements, making forays to find nectar. For weeks, they have hung, listless, with just the drab undersides of their wings showing. But now, they become more active, the flowers even becoming airborne in a blizzard of butterflies. And then, the Monarchs are off!

Gradually, they retrace their way northward, following the first blossoms of spring. In general, butterflies begin appearing in North America in March in southerly regions, and as late as July and August in more northern locales, such as Canada. Some hypothesize that the trigger for butterflies to begin their journeys northward from overwintering grounds is increased day length, but whatever the reason, the butterflies now become capable of reproducing. Arriving first in the southern United States, the migrants reproduce in late spring. Each succeeding generation works its way northward, so that by late July, the third generation will have reached Canada. However, it being so late in the season, these northern Monarchs only have enough time to produce one further generation, which is the one to make the long migration south.

How did all this long-distance travel come to be? One theory involves the primary larval food source, the milkweed plant. More than half of all North American milkweed species are native to Mexico. Some experts hold that the Monarch also evolved there. When the Ice Age ended, and the continental ice retreated northward, species of milkweed followed. With them came the Monarchs, gradually expanding their summer breeding range, but always returning to the warmth of their native origins for the winter.

Within the last 150 years, storm-tossed Monarchs have ranged as far as the Cape Verde Islands and Madeira in the Atlantic, and to most Pacific islands. Reaching New Zealand in about 1840, and Australia in 1870, they are now established and breeding in both countries. But in Europe, although there have been repeated sightings of individuals blown there by storms, there are no native species of milkweed, so Monarchs are unable to take up permanent residence. An interesting note is that the New Zealand population has already established communal overwintering sites in groves throughout the country.

Other butterflies also make mass directional flights, particularly in years of abundant reproduction. The Painted Lady, Great Southern White, Snout Butterfly, and many sulphurs make wide-ranging journeys. And the Gulf Fritillary, always appearing in Kansas between August and November, has been seen as far away as the Galapagos Islands and Argentina. From British Columbia south through California, the California Tortoiseshell flies in vast numbers high in the mountains. But none of these arrive at any fixed, repeated destination, as do the Monarchs. Nor do they make a return flight later, so most experts consider these flights wanderings, not true migration.

While it is true that all butterfly species go through the four stages of egg, caterpillar, pupa, and adult, each species has its own variations on the process. The familiar and well-loved Monarch may have one of the most interesting of life stories, but in your garden you will see many other species and witness the traits that give them their individuality. Each time you discover a new kind of bristly caterpillar lurking under a leaf, or glimpse an amorous pair of butterflies in their swirling nuptial flight, you'll be reminded again of the wonder of it all.

THREE

A PORTFOLIO OF BUTTERFLIES

There are a number of butterflies that, because they are common throughout the United States, exist in large numbers, and adapt very well to gardens, you may expect to see in your own garden. They are some of the most common species throughout the country, either because of sheer numbers, or because of their garden-adaptability.

The species listed are grouped in various families. There are six families we'll discuss here. The Brush-footed Butterflies (family Nymphalidae) include about one third of all North American butterflies; all have very short front legs. The Gossamer Wings (family Lycaenidae) include many small butterflies, such as the various blues. The Milkweed Butterflies (family Danaidae) comprise a large tribe worldwide whose larvae feed on species of milkweed plants; this group is most visibly represented by the Monarch. The Skippers (family Hesperiidae) are small, fast-moving butterflies that stay close to the ground. The Swallowtails (family Papilionidae) are characterized by protruding tails on the rear of each hindwing. Finally, the Whites (family Pieridae) are unassuming, commonly seen white or yellow species; they often feed on members of the mustard family. A good field guide will help you identify these and many other butterflies.

BRUSH-FOOTED BUTTERFLIES

Buckeye

Junonia coenia

Range: Found throughout the southern United States to California,
the Buckeye also spreads northward in summer.

Larval food: Among favorite edibles are *Linaria*, monkey flower
(*Mimulus*), snapdragon, and other members of
the figwort family (Scrophulariaceae). The buckeye also lives on
verbena and the common lawn weed, plantain.

Adult food: Members of the daisy family (Compositae),
buckwheat, mint, and plantain compose the adult diet.

Season: The Buckeye can be seen from March through October
in most regions, and all year long in the Deep South.

Habits: Common on non-manicured lawns where plantain is
allowed to grow, the buckeye is frequently found basking or "puddling,"
where its "eyespots" make it an easily identified species.
Males actively patrol an area, keeping a lookout for females.

Comma

Polygonia comma

~~~

Range: The Comma is found east of the Great Plains.
Larval food: Hops, nettles, and elms are larval staples.
Adult food: Butterfly bush, Michaelmas daisy, hebe, dandelion,
and sedum compose the adult diet.
Season: This distinctive species is prevalent from spring to fall.
Habits: An habitué of open woodlands and roadsides,
the Comma gets its common name from a curved silvery mark on the
underside of each hindwing. Caterpillars, which are
particularly fond of hops, fashion shelters from its leaves.

Great Spangled Fritillary

Speyeria cybele

Range: **This lovely species frequents the entire contiguous United States except Florida.**

Larval food: **Species of violet are the preferred food.**

Adult food: **Members of Compositae (particularly thistle),** *Monarda,* **vetch, verbena, and mountain laurel compose the adult diet.**

Season: **Taking flight from June to September, this species is easily recognized.**

Habits: **It is found in open woodlands and meadows and is the largest fritillary, with a calm, imperturbable manner demonstrated by its bobbing, floating flight and its lengthy visits at each flower.**

Gulf Fritillary

Agraulis vanillae

Range: While commonly found throughout the
southern United States and California,
Gulf Fritillary adults visit the middle states
in late summer.

Larval food: Species of passionflower compose the early diet.
Adult food: Lantana, daisy,
thistle, and passionflower draw adult diners.
Season: These resplendent orange-red butterflies
are common from early spring to late fall;
they are seen year-round in the Deep South.
Habits: This silver-speckled orange beauty is found
in abundance wherever passionflowers grow.
Males patrol the vines, in search of females.
They are easily adaptable to city life.

Milbert's Tortoise-shell

Aglais milberti

Range: **This species can be found through most of the northern United States.**
Larval food: **Nettles are the food of choice.**
Adult food: **Fruit juice, daisy, aster, goldenrod, ageratum, and other members of the composites family (Compositae) will draw this species. Lilac, wallflower, rock cress, and sedum are other attractants.**
Season: **Look for this species from March to November.**
Habits: **Although found in fields and forest verges, this butterfly adapts easily to gardens. Overwintering adults appear in earliest spring.**

Mourning Cloak

Nymphalis antiopa

Range: **This species ranges throughout the entire United States.**
Larval food: **Trees — such as willow, elm, poplar, aspen, cottonwood, birch, and hackberry — make up the larval diet.**
Adult food: **Fruit juice, butterfly bush, butterfly weed, pussy willow, and many members of Compositae draw them to the garden.**
Season: **Look for this large, striking butterfly year-round, including during warm spells in winter.**
Habits: **A creature of open woodlands and stream banks, the Mourning Cloak lives up to ten months, hibernating as an adult in hollow trees. It lays eggs in clusters; caterpillars feed communally at first, singly later. Despite its large size, the Mourning Cloak is a demure but elegant species that perches ornamentally.**

Painted Lady

Vanessa cardui

Range: It is a common sight throughout the entire United States.
Larval food: Many Compositae comprise the early diet,
including thistle, burdock, groundsel, and wormwood. Members of the borage and
mallow families, including hollyhock, are also consumed.
Adult food: A wide range of composites — plus mint, bee balm, butterfly bush,
privet, candytuft, wallflower, scabiosa, and sedum, among others — will lure this species.
Season: The Painted Lady is sighted from
May to October in the North and year-round in the South.
Habits: This denizen of meadows, fields, and even deserts often emigrates from the South
in large numbers during the summer. It is highly visible and adaptable to the garden.

Pearly Crescent-spot

Phyciodes tharos

Range: **East of the Rocky Mountains, the Pearly Crescentspot is a well-known butterfly.**

Larval food: **Michaelmas daisy and other species of *Aster* are preferred.**

Adult food: **Many Compositae, white clover, geranium, wallflower, butterfly weed, and mint attract this pretty species.**

Season: **It is seen from April to November in northern areas, but can be found year-round in the Deep South.**

Habits: **This species is an aggressive and highly visible habitué of meadows. Males actively patrol their territories and form "puddle clubs." The caterpillars feed communally.**

Question Mark

Polygonia interrogationis

Range: **East of the Rocky Mountains, this distinctive species is easily recognized.**
Larval food: **Nettle, hop, elm, and hackberry are preferred hosts.**
Adult food: **Fruit juice, aster, milkweed, and sweet pepperbush are all attractants.**
Season: **Look for it from spring through fall.**
Habits: **Similar in habits to the Comma, the Question Mark is recognized by a silver mark on the underside of the wings — the source of both its common and scientific names. It emigrates widely in late summer, sometimes in large groups; males bask and "puddle."**

Red Admiral

Vanessa atalanta

Range: **The entire contiguous United States is visited by this species.**

Larval food: **Nettle and hops are common meals.**

Adult food: **The Red Admiral's wide-ranging diet includes fruit juice, many members of Compositae, butterfly bush, milkweed, candytuft, alfalfa, sedum, wallflower, hebe, sweet pepperbush, fireweed, and mint.**

Season: **This species takes wing from April through October through most of its range, but is seen year-round in the Deep South.**

Habits: **At home in open woods and forest edges, gardens and parks, the Red Admiral is a gregarious butterfly. Males lurk in wait, darting out at females. Well-habituated to a garden environment, it is a prime consumer of nettles. Southerners migrate north in spring.**

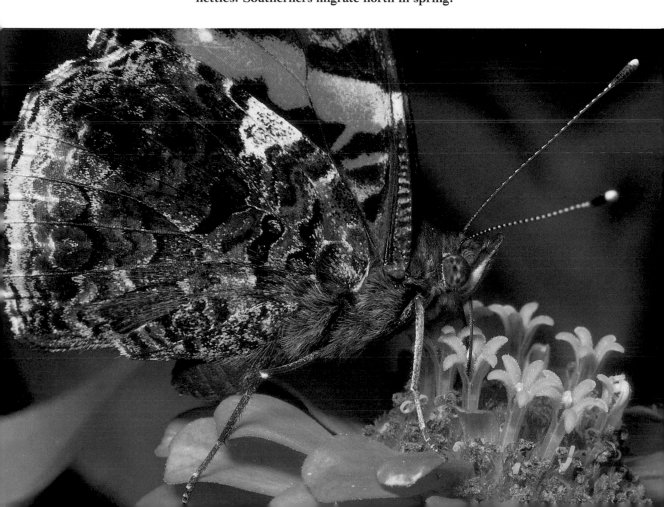

Red-spotted Purple

Basilarchia astyanax

Range: It is found throughout the United States east of the Rockies and in Arizona.

Larval food: Willow, aspen, poplar, cherry, plum, oak, hawthorn, apple, hornbeam, and gooseberry comprise the early diet.

Adult food: Fruit juice, viburnum, spirea, lilac, privet, and sweet pepperbush are favorites.

Season: March to October.

Habits: An inhabitant of woodland margins, stream banks, and meadows, the Red-spotted Purple often basks on roads and sidewalks, slowly flexing its brilliant-blue wings.

Viceroy

Basilarchia archippus

Range: The Viceroy can be found from the Great Basin eastward.

Larval food: Willow, aspen, poplar, apple, plum, and cherry are host plants.

Adult food: Fruit juice,

thistle, aster, Joe-Pye weed, goldenrod, and milkweed will attract this species.

Season: Viceroys usually fly from April to September.

Habits: A mimic of the offensive-tasting Monarch, or, in the South, the Queen, this butterfly displays similar behavior to the Red and White Admirals, and the Red-Spotted Purple, which are all closely related.

West Coast Lady

Vanessa annabella

Range: It is seen from the Great Plains to the Pacific.
Larval food: Nettles and members of the mallow family (Malvaceae) act as hosts.
Adult food: Butterfly bush, mallows, mints, and many members of Compositae will attract this species.
Season: Taking wing from early spring to late fall in most of its range, the West Coast Lady has an even longer flight period in the Southwest.
Habits: Often seen flitting through sun-dappled canyons and near creeks, the West Coast Lady is also fond of basking on streamside rocks and on open hilltops — often as communal activities.

White Admiral

Basilarchia arthemis

Range: **The northeastern United States
and Canada host this butterfly.**
Larval food: **This species favors birch, aspen, willow,
poplar, hawthorn, basswood, hornbeam, and shadblow.**
Adult food: **Fruit juice and a wide
range of flowers are preferred.**
Season: **Expect visits during high
summer, from June through August.**
Habits: **It is similar to the Red Admiral.
In fact, in certain areas where their
ranges overlap, the two species hybridize. The
caterpillar overwinters in a rolled-up leaf.**

Two views of the White Admiral, LEFT *and* ABOVE.

GOSSAMER WINGS

Brown Elfin

Incisalia augustinus

Range: This species inhabits the entire United States.
Larval food: In the East, members of the heath family (Ericaceae),
such as blueberry and azalea, comprise the diet. In the West,
ceanothus, apple, and the western heath family members salal, kinnikinick,
and madrona (*Arbutus menziesii*) are staples.
Adult food: It is partial to blueberry, cherry,
buckwheat, willow, kinnikinick, and plum.
Season: Brown Elfin takes flight from
April through June, but is most prominent in spring.
Habits: A frequent visitor to bogs, pine barrens, and other places where
the heath family grows, the Brown Elfin might also journey to urban areas
where host plants are grown.

Gray Hairstreak

Strymon melinus

Range: Occurring throughout the entire United States,
this species is also known as Common Hairstreak.
Larval food: Members of the pea and mallow families — including
clover, vetch, hollyhock, rose of Sharon, and hibiscus — are prime foods. Corn, mint,
oak, hawthorn, strawberry, and the ever-popular hops are also consumed.
Adult food: Sweet clover, goldenrod, plumbago, mint, Queen Anne's
lace, and milkweed comprise a varied diet.
Season: Broods take flight from April to October.
Habits: One of America's most prevalent species, due to its
wide range of acceptable food sources, the Gray
Hairstreak prefers open meadows, fields, and chaparral. Highly territorial
males dart from cover after females or intruding males.

Gray Hairstreak, RIGHT.

Silvery Blue

Glaucopsyche lygdamus

Range: Throughout the United States, the beautifully colored Silvery Blue can be easily identified.

Larval food: It uses members of the pea family (Fabaceae) as host plants.

Adult food: Members of Compositae — such as coneflower — cherry, and lupine are preferred.

Season: This species appears from March through July.

Habits: Open woodlands, stream banks, fields, and mountain meadows harbor this butterfly. It is an early riser that is garden-adaptable. Ants seem to guard the caterpillars in exchange for sweet "honeydew" exuded by the larvae.

Spring Azure

Celastrina ladon

Range: This species is known throughout the entire United States.

Larval food: Dogwood, ceanothus, viburnum, cherry, and blueberry are species of nourishment.

Adult food: It feeds on a number of flowers, including privet, lilac, holly, ceanothus, rock cress, escallonia, cotoneaster, milkweed, willow, spicebush, dandelion, violet, and cherry.

Season: Watch for this species from January to October, depending on the region.

Habits: The Spring Azure frequents freshwater marshes, fields, forest edges, and parks. It makes a good garden specimen, usually found in early spring. The males are actively territorial.

Spring Azure, LEFT.

MILKWEED BUTTERFLIES

Monarch

Danaus plexippus

~

Range: Its territory encompasses all of the United States except the northwest corner.
Larval food: Milkweed is the preferred host.
Adult food: Milkweed, butterfly bush, goldenrod, Joe-Pye weed, gayfeather, tithonia, cosmos, abelia, lilac, lantana, mallow, and mint are all attractants.
Season: Successive broods emerge from spring to fall.
Habits: The Monarch is the only butterfly to truly migrate to and from overwintering spots. It is also the most readily identifiable butterfly in the country. If America had a national butterfly, this would undoubtedly be it.

SKIPPERS

Tawny-edged Skipper

Polites themistocles

Range: **Most of the United States, excluding some areas of the Northwest, is the domain of this tiny butterfly.**
Larval food: **Grasses, including lawn grasses, are host plants.**
Adult food: **Its varied diet includes thistle, red clover, alfalfa, chicory, purple coneflower, sweet alyssum, and lantana.**
Season: **Broods take flight from April through September, depending on region.**
Habits: **This species is a common denizen of parks and other grassy places. As it is not a lawn pest, welcome this sprightly orange miniature to your garden.**

SWALLOWTAILS

Giant Swallowtail

Heraclides cresphontes

Range: Most of the central and southern United States is within this butterfly's realm.

Larval food: Species of citrus, plus prickly-ash and Hercules'-club (*Zanthoxylum* spp.), hop tree (*Ptelea trifoliata*), and rue are favorites.

Adult food: It is drawn to lantana, honeysuckle, milkweed, lilac, goldenrod, citrus blossoms, azalea, and dame's rocket.

Season: The Giant Swallowtail is found year-round in the South, and from May to September farther north.

Habits: Groves, forest edges, and stream banks are the home of this, North America's largest butterfly. Caterpillars, called "orange dogs," are sometimes plentiful on citrus.

A close-up, OPPOSITE, *shows the iridescent patterning of the Giant Swallowtail's wings.*

Pipevine Swallowtail

Battus philenor

Range: **Most of the United States
is inhabited by this species.**
Larval food: **As its common name would indicate,
species of pipevine (*Aristolochia*) are the principal host plants.**
Adult food: **It feeds on thistle, lilac, honeysuckle,
milkweed, butterfly bush, phlox, bee balm,
dame's rocket, petunia, and fruit-tree blossoms.**
Season: **The Pipevine Swallowtail can be
observed from January to November, depending on the region.**
Habits: **It inhabits woodland clearings, roadsides,
and meadows. Unpalatable to birds, this
species is mimicked by several other swallowtail species.**

Spicebush Swallowtail

Pterourus troilus

Range: This species roves east of the Rockies.
Larval food: Spicebush, sassafras,
tulip tree (**Liriodendron tulipifera**), sweet bay
(**Magnolia virginiana**), and prickly-ash are hosts.
Adult food: Honeysuckle, thistle, milkweed,
clover, Joe-Pye weed, lantana, sweet
pepperbush, and mimosa draw this lovely butterfly.
Season: Flight periods occur from April to October.
Habits: Found in woodlands, meadows, and
pine barrens, this mimic of the Pipevine
Swallowtail is an inveterate "puddler."

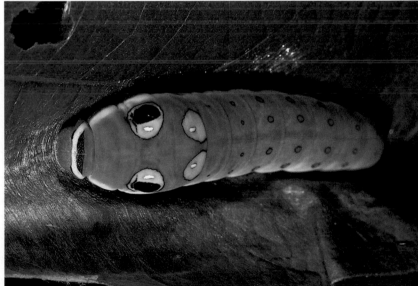

Tiger Swallowtail

Pterourus glaucus

Range: More wide-ranging than any other swallowtail, this species is found east of the Rockies.
Larval food: Its varied early diet includes cherry, ash, birch, aspen, cottonwood, tulip tree, willow, sweet bay, hop tree, spicebush, lilac, and hornbeam.
Adult food: Butterfly bush, thistle, milkweed, honeysuckle, phlox, Joe-Pye weed, abelia, bee balm, and dandelion all lure this species.
Season: Its flight season begins in early spring and ends in late fall.
Habits: Parks, woods, and orchards are home to this common butterfly. The dark females mimic the Pipevine Swallowtail.

WHITES

Cabbage White
Artogeia rapae

Range: It is well known throughout the entire United States and most of Canada.

Larval food: The Cabbage White feeds on members of the mustard family (Brassicaceae) including cabbage and its relatives as well as on cress, wallflower, and members of the caper family, such as *Cleome.*

Adult food: Mustard, wallflower, rock cress, dandelion, aster, mint, lantana, and many others are mealtime favorites.

Season: This species takes wing from early spring to late fall.

Habits: This common butterfly calls open woods, fields, vacant lots, and vegetable gardens home. Introduced in the nineteenth century, it is now our most widely occurring species.

Common Sulphur

Colias philodice

Range: This species occurs throughout the entire United States north of Florida.

Larval food: Members of the pea family (Fabaceae), such as alfalfa,
clover, vetch, and lupine, are early diet staples.

Adult food: Clover, goldenrod, dandelion, tithonia, milkweed, and phlox entice this butterfly.

Season: Look for it from early spring to late fall.

Habits: The Common Sulphur congregates at puddles in large groups. It also frequents
vegetable gardens and lawns, as well as fields, roadsides, and meadows.

FOUR

CAPTIVATING FLOWERS AND PLANTS FOR THE BUTTERFLY

Just what kinds of flowers do butterflies find enticing? In a garden overflowing with gorgeous blooms, what prompts a butterfly to prefer one flower over all the rest? The choice is somewhat determined by butterfly anatomy. The organ for taking up nectar, the proboscis, is a tube, like a soda straw, that can be conveniently coiled up when not in use. Therefore, the most appropriate nectar source will also be tubular. But since butterflies have proboscis lengths in proportion to their body sizes, not all flowers are suitable for all butterflies. A one-inch skipper would be at a loss at how to cope with some of the large-flowered sages. But these flowers suit a swallowtail perfectly.

Butterflies are among the largest insects you're likely to encounter. They are also exceedingly long-legged. So a commodious platform on which to alight is important. Small butterflies, such as skippers and blues, have no problem coming and going from ground-hugging plants, such as thyme or sweet alyssum, but the larger swallowtails and others need taller, sturdier perches to afford plenty of landing leeway. Many of the best butterfly flowers are not single blossoms, but clusters of numerous small blossoms, arranged in a horizontal plane, such as Queen Anne's lace or yarrow. This type of blossom also saves butterfly energy. A butterfly can load up on the nectar of many individual blossoms from one vantage point, without having to flit from blossom to blossom.

Most members of the Compositae (or Daisy) family are ideal butterfly flowers. In fact, these plants co-evolved with insects. Composites take their name from the fact that what we think of as a single daisy-type flower is in reality a collection of dozens of tiny individual florets. Look closely. Densely clustered in the center are the tiny "disc flowers." These are surrounded by "ray flowers," each having what appears to be a petal attached. The ray flowers make the flower larger and therefore more noticeable to a potential pollenizer, as well as furnishing ample landing space.

Fragrance is also a quality of a good butterfly flower, and butterflies generally visit flowers in descending order of fragrance strength. Luckily, butterflies are usually attracted by scents that we also enjoy, so many of our favorite plants — heliotropes, viburnums, lilacs — are good choices for your butterfly garden. But this is not necessarily the case with other pollenizers. Many plants emit the odor of rotting flesh to attract the carrion flies that are their pollenizers. Bird-pollinated flowers tend to be scentless, most coming from high altitudes, particularly the mountains of Central and South America, where it is too cool for insect pollenizers. Birds can create their own body heat, and so they are the primary pollinators at such heights. Scent travels little in such cold air, so flowers rely on purely visual attractiveness. Since

Planted together in this garden, ABOVE, *red poppies, flat-topped yellow yarrow,*
golden Heliopsis, *small but profuse mexican daisy,*
and the spires of lamb's ear offer dining variety for butterflies.

birds discern red most easily, and their bills are long enough to reach into a variety of flowers, a "bird flower" is characteristically red, tubular, and scentless. Often, the blooms are arranged on a stalk so that the individual blossoms all face the same way, affording easy access for a hovering

white, to increase visibility in what little light there is, and are tubular or trumpet-shaped to accommodate moths' often long proboscises.

Because of the butterfly's sensitivity to full-spectrum and ultraviolet light, flower color plays a significant role in attracting these creatures. Since you'll

Easy-care red valerian attracts many sorts of butterflies, while the columbine and poker flowers lure hummingbirds to this informal corner of the garden.

hummingbird. Moth-pollinated flowers, on the other hand, tend to be some of the most heavily scented. In the dark of night, when moths are active, a far-reaching perfume is a great advantage. Most "moth flowers" are also

probably want to lure the greatest number of species possible to your garden, a variety of flowers or a "something for everyone" approach is a good idea. An assortment of plant heights, sizes and colors of flowers, and changes in seasonal bloom will bring many species to frequent your garden.

Remember, since you are trying to suit your garden to the butterflies that occur naturally in your area, you'll want to include a certain number of native plants. Many natives are quite appealing, so the beauty of your garden shouldn't suffer. In fact, several natives are true garden stars. Gay-feather, Michaelmas daisy, and butterfly weed are not only all first-rate butterfly plants, but also border favorites, with many cultivated varieties to choose from. Natives are even more important if you choose to provide food sources for caterpillars. Adult butterflies are less specific in their food requirements, finding many "foreign" plants acceptable for their nectar needs. But, not having the mobility of the winged adults, caterpillars often require specific plants for food.

Some less finicky caterpillars, such as the Buckeye, Painted Lady, Comma, and Mourning Cloak, will eat a wide variety of food plants. But Monarchs definitely prefer milkweed, whites choose members of the mustard family, and sulphurs like clover. Some of the most specific are the Pipevine Swallowtail, whose caterpillars feed on the Dutchman's pipe; the Anise Swallowtail, which prefers fennel; and the Spicebush Swallowtail, whose food source is the highly aromatic spicebush.

If your aim is to attract some of the butterflies that are specific to your area, consult a local entomologist or one of the butterfly organizations listed in the Appendices. They will help you with appropriate food and nectar sources for your garden, be they native or acceptable "exotics."

The following plant lists include trees, shrubs, herbaceous perennials, annuals, biennials, and vines that adult butterflies or their caterpillars prefer. In general, these plants attract many species of butterfly. Mention is made of any butterflies that are particularly attracted to a certain type of plant, whether it's as a nectar source for the adult, or as a food source for the caterpillar. To my knowledge, there are no plants that are actually harmful to butterflies, or that are inordinately enticing to butterfly predators.

The plants mentioned are not merely those that butterflies are fond of, but also those that are beautiful in their own right. You will find them listed alphabetically by common name, and organized by height and season of bloom to aid you in composing your "garden picture." Hardiness is given according to USDA hardiness zones (see page 142). Because you may also wish to invite moths or hummingbirds into your garden, after the butterfly plants are lists of some flowers that these creatures will find to their liking.

TREES

Trees are used by butterflies mostly as larval food sources, and rarely for nectar. In many instances, a variety of butterflies are adapted to using the same tree, so a small garden with one or two trees may accommodate many different butterflies.

Birch *Betula* spp.

Fast-growing deciduous trees, many birches are noted for their white bark or graceful branching habits. They make interesting garden elements in winter as well as summer. *B. jacquemontii* is the whitest, while the bark of the canoe birch, *B. papyrifera,* an American native, peels in curly sheets. They make a lovely display of yellow fall foliage. Hardy throughout the country. Especially attractive to: Mourning Cloak, White Admiral, Tiger Swallowtail, and Western Tiger Swallowtail.

Dogwood *Cornus* spp.

C. florida, a southeastern native, comes in many forms, with blossoms ranging from snowy white to carmine; some have variegated foliage. It is a horizontally spreading tree, growing to twenty feet tall and displaying deep-red fall foliage. Hardy to Zone 6. Especially attractive to: Spring Azure.

Elm *Ulmus* spp.

Medium to large deciduous (*U. parvifolia* keeps its leaves in warm-winter areas) trees, all the elms are fast-growing. Most, unfortunately, are subject to Dutch elm disease, but are worth a try in the West. Hardy in all zones. Especially attractive to: Comma, Mourning Cloak, and Question Mark.

Hackberry *Celtis* spp.

Deciduous elm relatives, the hackberries are deep-rooting trees, good for narrow planting strips and for gardening beneath. They tolerate heat, drought, wind, and alkaline soil, growing to thirty to forty feet. One or another species is adaptable to any hardiness zone. Especially attractive to: Hackberry Butterfly and Question Mark.

Hawthorn *Crataegus* spp.

Small deciduous trees, the hawthorns boast flowers in shades from white through deep rose, followed by abundant scarlet or black berries, which are relished by birds. There are many species and varieties to choose from. Hardy to Zone 2. Especially attractive to: Red-spotted Purple, White Admiral, and Gray Hairstreak.

The larvae of many species of butterflies feed on the leaves of the eastern dogwood, shown here in its pink-flowered form, LEFT.

Hornbeam *Carpinus* spp.

C. caroliniana, an American native, reaches thirty feet, and provides a nice fall foliage show. *C. betulus,* the European counterpart, has a form, 'Fastigiata', with a narrow column in youth; it becomes more pyramidal at maturity. Hardy to Zone 3. Especially attractive to: Red-spotted Purple and White Admiral.

One of the many hawthorns suitable for the garden grows, ABOVE. *More are native to the United States than anywhere else. Accordingly, they provide food for caterpillars of several butterfly species. The large, flat clusters of this viburnum,* OPPOSITE, *are composed of dozens of tiny, nectar-filled blossoms.*

Orange, Lemon, and Related Species
Citrus spp.

Evergreen trees, the citrus species range in size from twenty feet down to dwarfs, which are suitable for containers. The ambrosially scented blossoms are followed by decorative or edible fruits. Hardy in Zones 9–10. Especially attractive to: Giant Swallowtail.

Poplar, Aspen, and Cottonwood *Populus* spp.

Fast-growing deciduous trees, *Populus* species are at their most beautiful in the fall, when they display brilliant-yellow foliage. Surface roots and suckers are a potential problem. Bees gather the sweet-scented resin (balsam) from newly emerging leaves to use in a substance for patching their hives. Hardy in all zones. Especially attractive to: Mourning Cloak, Viceroy, Tiger Swallowtail, and Western Tiger Swallowtail.

Willow *Salix* spp.

Very fast-growing (but not long-lived) deciduous trees, many willows grow in wet areas and bear white "pussies" (anthers on male trees) in early spring. If you plunge a pencil-thick branch into moist soil, you can create a new tree. Hardy in all zones. Especially attractive to: Mourning Cloak, Red-spotted Purple, Viceroy, and Tiger Swallowtail.

SHRUBS

Spring-blooming

TALL

California Lilac
Ceanothus spp.

The small, evergreen leaves of the California lilac are hidden by masses of clustered, tiny, true-blue flowers. *C. veitchianus,* 'Julia Phelps', and 'Victoria' are the hardiest, to Zone 8. All need good drainage, preferring no water in summer. Very fast-growing, this shrub is a good bank-holder. Especially attractive to: For larval food — Spring Azure and Brown Elfin. For nectar — many.

Lilac *Syringa vulgaris*

There are hundreds of lilacs to choose from. Although most require winter chill, Descanso hybrids are adapted to warm-winter areas. Once they have bloomed in spring, lilacs become uninteresting in summer, so train a clematis or other vine into them for a longer season of interest. Hardy to Zone 2. Especially attractive to: For larval food — Tiger Swallowtail. For nectar — Milbert's Tortoiseshell, Monarch, Giant Swallowtail, and Pipevine Swallowtail.

Viburnum *Viburnum* spp.

Evergreen *V. tinus* and deciduous *V.* × *bodnantense* 'Dawn' bloom during warm spells in winter, of value to Mourning Cloak and other early-risers. Among the many species, *V.* × *burkwoodii, V. carlesii,* and *V.* × *carlcephalum* are all sweetly fragrant. Hardy to Zone 4. Especially attractive to: For larval food — Spring Azure.

MEDIUM

Bridal Wreath *Spiraea* spp.

This genus consists of deciduous natives and Asian species. *S. thunbergii* makes an effort in warm winter spells. *S.* × *vanhouttei* bears profuse flowers on its mounded, arching branches. Hardy to Zone 2. Especially attractive to: Red-spotted Purple.

Carmel Creeper
Ceanothus griseus vars.

This spreading evergreen shrub rewards gardeners with striking blue flowers. Hardy to Zone 8. Especially attractive to: For larval food — Spring Azure. For leaves — California Hairstreak.

Mexican Orange
Choisya ternata

This glossy-leaved evergreen is attractive year-round. It becomes smothered with citrus-scented white flowers and is fairly drought-tolerant. Hardy to Zone 8.

Rockrose *Cistus* spp.

Evergreen Mediterranean natives, the rockroses display white to bright-rose crinkled-crepe flowers that resemble single roses, often with a ruby spot at each petal base. The rockroses have many other attributes: they grow quickly, do not need frequent summer watering, and are even flame retardant! Hardy to Zone 7.

Native to the Mediterranean, rockrose opens its crepe-textured blossoms above fuzzy gray leaves, RIGHT. *It is ideal for mild areas of the summer-dry West.*

TALL

Arrowwood
Viburnum dentatum

This tough deciduous native grows to ten-plus feet. Its white flowers are followed by bright-blue berries, with respectable fall foliage. Hardy to Zone 2.

Buckeye *Aesculus* spp.

Deciduous natives, the buckeyes often reach tree proportions. They bear beautiful palmate leaves and clustered "torches" of small white to glowing red flowers. They will take some shade. Hardy to Zone 5.

Butterfly Bush
Buddleia davidii

This appropriately named fast-growing deciduous shrub reaches heights of ten feet. Lovely gray-green leaves are complemented by wands of white or purple scented flowers, and looks best if cut to two feet in spring. Hardy to Zone 5.

Cotoneaster
Cotoneaster spp.

Evergreen or deciduous workhorse shrubs, the cotoneasters are most noted for winter berries. *C. lacteus* has graceful, willowy form and is lovely in informal hedges. Prune this plant selectively, but do not shear. Hardy to Zone 7. *C. racemiflorus soongoricus* has shiny green leaves, pink blossoms, and berries on an eight-foot shrub. Hardy to Zone 3.

Mock Orange
Philadelphus spp.

Multitudes of snow-white, one- to one-and-a-half-inch, golden-centered flowers weight the arched branches of the mock orange. It exudes a scent of orange blossoms. Best used as a screening plant, it is somewhat plain when out of bloom. Single flowers are more useful to butterflies than are double ones. Hardy to Zone 2.

Lilac *Syringa* spp.

Aside from the common lilac, there are many other later-blooming species and hybrids derived from them, most with graceful, arching panicles of pink to violet blossoms. Those developed by Isabella Preston in Canada are among the loveliest, as well as being zone hardy. Especially attractive to: Painted Lady and Red-spotted Purple.

Spicebush *Lindera benzoin*

Not an overwhelmingly ornamental shrub; spicebush is best used in woodland plantings. It is a prime food source for the larval Spicebush Swallowtail. Greenish flowers are a nectar source for Spring Azure. Hardy to Zone 6.

<u>MEDIUM</u>

Bush Cinquefoil

Potentilla fruticosa

Deciduous, tough, and a vigorous native of mountains of the entire Northern Hemisphere, the bush cinquefoils delight gardeners and butterflies alike. Most have yellow (some orange, scarlet, pink, or white) blossoms, resembling small single roses, which spangle the twiggy branches from late spring through fall. Hardy to Zone 2.

Dwarf Butterfly Bush

Buddleia davidii Nanhoensis

A scaled-down version of typical butterfly bush, recommended types are red-violet 'Petit Plum' and blue-violet 'Petit Indigo'. See butterfly bush for additional information.

Glossy Abelia

Abelia × grandiflora

This fast-growing evergreen has arching branches decked with white or pale-lilac scented tubular flowers. It is a trouble-free plant and is quite drought-resistant. Hardy to Zone 7.

Hebe *Hebe* spp.

These New Zealand natives grow best along the Pacific Coast. Neat, evergreen, fast-growing, and floriferous, the various species and hybrids bloom from February to December, with a peak in midsummer. Their tiny flowers grow in elongated clusters, often opening one color and fading to another, for a two-toned effect. Hardy to Zone 8.

Privet *Ligustrum* spp.

Sturdy evergreen or semi-deciduous, the privets are most often used for hedges or screens. Like lilacs, to which they are closely related, they are irresistible to butterflies. Hardy in Zones 2–10, depending on the variety. Especially attractive to: Painted Lady, Red-spotted Purple, and Spring Azure.

Spirea *Spiraea* spp.

S. × bumalda and its derivatives have ideal, flat-topped clusters of raspberry pink, white, or whimsical mixtures of both colors, as with 'Shirobana'. As they bloom on new wood, prune hard in spring to stimulate growth. Hardy to Zone 3. Especially attractive to: Red-spotted Purple.

The scented pale lilac bells of glossy abelia, OPPOSITE, *bloom for months on end.*

Germander
Teucrium chamaedrys

An Evergreen subshrub, germander endures poor, rocky soil, but needs good drainage. It can be clipped to create a low hedge and displays purple or white flowers. Hardy to Zone 5.

Hebe *Hebe* spp.

As with the medium-height *Hebe* species, these lovely shrubs grow quickly and flower abundantly. There are many prostrate to eighteen-inch varieties. Some of these are the hardiest, to Zone 7.

Lavender *Lavandula* spp.

Look forward to grayish evergreen mounds topped by wiry wands tipped with sweet-scented white, pink, lavender(!), or purple blossoms. As a bonus, they are drought- and insect-resistant. Hardy in Zones 7–10 (but they grow so fast, they can be used as annuals).

Lavender Cotton
Santolina spp.

Don't be misled by the common name: The common species, *S. chamaecyparissus*, has a certain resemblance to lavender, but the blossoms are bright- to pale-yellow buttons. *S. virens* has greener leaves, and lemon polka-dot flowers. Hardy to Zone 5.

Late summer and fall

TALL

Chaste Tree

Vitex agnus-castus

Attractive palmate foliage and branches tipped with seven-inch spikes of lavender-blue flowers distinguish the chaste tree, a valuable late nectar source. Hardy to Zone 5.

Rose of Sharon

Hibiscus syriacus

This deciduous shrub is late to leaf out but has a long season of bloom, decked with white, pink, or red flowers resembling those of tropical hibiscus or hollyhock. Of the many kinds available, the ones with single flowers appeal more to butterflies than do the doubles. Hardy to Zone 6. Especially attractive to: Gray Hairstreak.

Sweet Pepperbush

Clethra spp.

A deciduous, colonizing native, the sweet pepperbush bears clusters of deliciously fragrant blossoms in August. It thrives in moist soil. The pink form, 'Rosea', is particularly nice. Hardy to Zone 3. Especially attractive to: Red-spotted Purple, Question Mark, and Spicebush Swallowtail.

LOW

Bluebeard *Caryopteris* spp.

Gray-green leaves are complemented by clusters of small dusty-blue flowers at every branch tip on this diminutive plant. It is as attractive to butterflies, on a smaller scale, as *Buddleia*. It is also quite drought-tolerant. Hardy to Zone 4.

Hebe *Hebe* 'Autumn Glory'

This hebe is similar to others, but has claret new leaves and stems. Its clear violet flowers begin their display in midsummer and peak in October. Hardy to Zone 7.

Old-fashioned lavender, OPPOSITE, *thrives in sunshine and good drainage, furnishing nectar for butterflies and sachets for linens. The lovely chaste tree, on the other hand, thrives on neglect,* ABOVE.

HERBACEOUS PERENNIALS

Spring

Aubrieta *Aubrieta* spp.

A mat-forming evergreen, aubrieta is the classic (to the point of cliché) companion of *Arabis, Iberis,* and *Aurinia* in rockeries. The flowers are often a screaming magenta, so seek out subtler shades of periwinkle or rose. It is tough and long-suffering. Hardy to Zone 3. Especially attractive to: Cabbage White.

Basket-of-Gold
Aurinia saxatilis

Sprawly mounds of grayish evergreen leaves, to six inches, are covered with billows of tiny yellow flowers on this charming plant. The typical form is a harsh yellow, and when combined with strident shades of *Aubrieta* or creeping phlox, it creates the visual equivalent of fingernails on a blackboard. 'Citrina' and 'Silver Queen', however, are a more tender shade, blending well with nearly everything. Hardy to Zone 5. Especially attractive to: Cabbage White and spring-active butterflies.

Creeping Phlox
Phlox stolonifera

Another evergreen mat-former of easy disposition, creeping phlox is blanketed with white, periwinkle, pink, or rose blossoms. It spreads modestly in well-drained locations. Hardy to Zone 3. Especially attractive to: All smaller spring butterflies.

Evergreen Candytuft
Iberis sempervirens

Completely covered with sparkling white flowers for many weeks, evergreen candytuft is also enhanced by narrow needlelike foliage. Clip back after bloom for bushiness and to produce additional flowers. It is another trouble-free, durable, mustard-family member. Hardy to Zone 6. Especially attractive to: Wide range of early butterflies.

Jacob's Ladder
Polemonium spp.

Dwarf pink and blue varieties of this charming flower begin in April in some species, followed in late May by tall blue or white *P. caeruleum.* All have half-inch flowers of silken texture, set off by a central golden point of stamens, as well as lovely pinnate foliage. They appreciate sun or light shade. Hardy to Zone 4.

Although meadow rue, RIGHT, *will grow where its name indicates, you'll get three times as many fluffy flowers with proper garden care.*

Meadow Rue
Thalictrum spp.

Covered with ferny foliage like its columbine relatives, meadow rue grows much taller, some to seven feet. From May on, flowers appear either in large fluffy-looking clusters (white, yellow, or lavender) above the foliage, or in masses of small lavender bells with cream stamens dangling from delicate-looking branched panicles. The former, including *T. aquilegifolium, T. flavum,* and *T. polygamum,* invite more butterflies. Hardy to Zone 3. Especially attractive to: Swallowtails.

Mexican Daisy
Erigeron karvinskianus

This low evergreen has the same dimensions and culture as *Aurinia,* but sports small white daisies, pink in bud, which decorate the plant nearly year-round. The Mexican daisy spreads mildly underground and self-sows. It is useful in pavements and on steep rocky banks or walls. Its long season makes it popular with a wide range of butterflies. Hardy to Zone 7 as a perennial; a self-sown annual nearly anywhere.

Pinks *Dianthus plumarius*

These clove-scented small carnation relatives have blue-gray evergreen foliage, which makes them classic edging plants. 'Allwood' strain is particularly long-blooming. Some older varieties date to Elizabethan times. A diverse selection of colors encompasses shades of white through red and plum; the petals might also be striped, speckled, or lacy-edged. Hardy to Zone 5. Especially attractive to: Painted Lady.

Rock Cress *Arabis* spp.

The rock cresses are low-growing plants for use as ground covers, on planted pavement, or in rock gardens. Gardeners will appreciated the foliage, which is variegated in some varieties and is pretty year-round. The flowers are white, pink, or rose. Hardy to Zone 2. Especially attractive to: Cabbage White and other early-risers.

Sea Kale *Crambe maritima*

An outstanding foliage plant, sea kale has large, rippled, glaucous leaves, topped off in May by a two-foot branched panicle of white flowers. Hardy to Zone 6. Especially attractive to: whites.

Sea Pink *Armeria* spp.

Tufted evergreen foliage and red, pink, or white flower heads perched on wiry stems make sea pink look like a combination of grass and clover. It blooms spring through fall, even when neglected. This plant is best located near paving, or where foliage won't get confused with lawn. Dwarf varieties derived from *A. maritima* grow to eight inches; *A. pseudarmeria* is larger in every dimension, to twenty inches. Hardy to Zone 5. Especially attractive to: Skippers, blues, and other smaller butterflies.

Wallflower

Cheiranthus and *Erysimum* spp.

These two genera are similar and confused in the nomenclature. They are evergreen members of the mustard family, as so many early-blooming plants tend to be, with characteristic four-petaled flowers arranged in erect wands. Often suffused with the fragrance of violets, they bloom in white through shades of yellow, rose, purple, and scarlet, and old-fashioned shades of murky maroon and mahogany. Some are even striped. True to their name, they will grow in chinks in a wall, or on a bank. They prefer cool-summer areas, such as New England and the Pacific Coast. Hardy to Zone 5. Especially attractive to: Cabbage White and spring-active butterflies.

Favored by many nectar-feeding insects as well as hummingbirds, scarlet and pink bee balm are backed by moth-attracting flowering tobacco, OPPOSITE.

Astilbe

Astilbe × arendsii

Clumping plants with handsome foliage, astilbes are topped by plumes of white through pink and red. There are many named varieties, mostly with upright inflorescences. 'Ostrich Plume', however, nods gracefully. Hardy to Zone 2. Especially attractive to: Monarch and Painted Lady.

Bee Balm *Monarda* spp.

The tousled heads of bee balm's tubular mint-type flowers top three-foot stems arising from colonizing basal leaves. Named varieties come in pink, scarlet, white, and a dusty mahogany. Make sure these have been vegetatively propagated, as most seed-grown plants turn out mauve. The fragrant leaves make a pleasant tea. Hardy to Zone 3.

Bellflower *Campanula* spp.

Encompassing dozens of variations of lavender-blue, white, or, rarely, pink, bellflowers grow in bell or cup shapes. Most bloom profusely and are of easy culture, some of the petite rock-garden types being the exception. *C. persicifolia, C. carpatica, C. glomerata, C. lactiflora, C. latiloba, C. trachelium, C. alliariifolia,* and their varieties are charming border plants. *C. poscharskyana, C. portenschlagiana, C. raddeana, C. cochleariifolia,* and *C. rotundifolia* are good in stone walls, or rockeries of the free-and-easy sort. Avoid, like the plague, *C. rapunculoides.* This lovely habitué of alleyways and abandoned farms is an ineradicable thug. Bellflowers of the more open and erect type are more conducive to butterfly feasting. Most are very hardy, with some appropriate to all zones.

Blanketflower
Gaillardia × *grandiflora*

These bright and bountiful daisies are the result of hybrids between two prairie natives, one of which, being an annual, unfortunately shortens their life expectancy. The petals are shades of red or yellow, often zoned concentrically, set off by maroon-red centers, and they range from six inches ('Goblin') to two feet ('Yellow Queen'). Hardy in all zones. Especially attractive to: Comma, Painted Lady, Red Admiral, Question Mark, and Viceroy.

Border Phlox
Phlox hybrids

Stately queens of the border, phlox come in nearly every color imaginable. Sweetly scented and durable, no garden is complete without some, with which your butterfly visitors will quickly agree. Some of the best are 'Mt. Fuji' (white), 'Dodo Hanbury Forbes' (clear pink), and 'Gaiety' (bright red). Hardy to Zone 2. Especially attractive to: Tiger Swallowtail, Red Admiral, and Viceroy.

Border Pincushion Flower *Scabiosa caucasica*

Another of the top-ten doers, border pincushion flowers flourish from late spring until hard frost. They sport frilled two-inch blossoms in shades of lavender-blue or white nodding atop two-and-a-half-foot wiry stems. Two of the best varieties are 'Fama' (nearly true-blue) and 'Miss Wilmott' (sparkling white). They are superb for cutting, too. Hardy to Zone 5.

Butterfly Weed
Asclepias tuberosa

Butterfly weed is not so called for nothing. Striking orange flowers, which appear summer through early fall, attract every butterfly within miles; these creatures seem to materialize out of thin air when butterfly weed is blooming. A must for the butterfly garden, this plant is hardy in all zones. Other species, all of them natives, have flowers of pink and purple, and are equally alluring to your winged guests.

Common Valerian
Valeriana officinalis

Despite being rather rank-growing, this plant is one of the most attractive to butterflies. Try to find a less refined area where it can romp about, flaunting its flat-topped heads of tiny pale-pink flowers for all winged comers. Hardy to Zone 3.

Crambe *Crambe cordifolia*

By no means a duplication of the spring-blooming *C. maritima*, this crambe consists of a mound of eighteen-inch coarse green leaves, from which rises an enormous branched panicle — easily six feet by six feet — consisting of thousands of tiny white flowers. The effect is that of a Brobdingnagian baby's-breath. After the flowers drop, the stems and seedpods create an airy mass of celadon, later taking on purplish tinges, so don't be over-eager to cut them down. In the plant's native steppes of Central Asia, these stems break off at the base and become probably the world's largest tumbleweeds! Make sure to place this plant where you really want it. If you move it, the pieces of root left behind will produce new plants. Despite its size, its delicacy warrants a place even in small gardens. Hardy to Zone 4, at least. Especially attractive to: Milbert's Tortoiseshell, Mourning Cloak, and Painted Lady.

Butterfly weed is a lovely, long-lasting plant that can grow to three feet high, RIGHT. *Its flat, orange, red, and sometimes yellow flower clusters make striking garden accents and are sure to attract an abundance of delicate winged visitors.*

Cupid's Dart

Catananche caerulea

Foot-tall blue flowers — which at first glance resemble bachelor's-buttons — bearing silver, papery bracts characterize this plant. The flowers bloom over a long period, and dry quite well. Good drainage is a requirement. Hardy to Zone 2. Especially attractive to: Viceroy, Painted Lady, and Great Spangled Fritillary.

Dame's Rocket

Hesperis matronalis

A European native, dame's rocket has been beloved for centuries. It would be hard to improve on the simple charm of their four-foot white to lavender-purple wands of flowers, which suggest a cross between a sweet William and a single stock, and are every bit as sweetly scented. They are a perfect cottage plant, self-sowing generously, but not pestiferously, thriving on neglect. Hardy to Zone 3. Especially attractive to: Painted Lady, Cabbage White, various swallowtails, and Monarch.

Garden Sage

Salvia × *superba*

A mild-tempered clumper, garden sage is usually represented by the German varieties 'Ost Friesland' and 'Mainacht' ('May Night'). Their erect spikes of rich purple bloom for many weeks. If they're cut back and fed when the first show is over, you'll get a second bloom, Hardy to Zone 5. Especially attractive to: Buckeye, Red Admiral, Silvery Blue, and Common Sulphur.

Gayfeather *Liatris* spp.

A very un-daisy-like Composite, gayfeather grows from an underground tuber. It rises like a poker covered with button-buds of white or mauve, opening, from the top down, into tousled, fluffy florets. An American native, the Dutch have developed and been selling them back to us as cut flowers for several years. Grow your own, and feed some butterflies in the bargain. Hardy to Zone 3.

Gazania *Gazania* spp.

These six-inch-high South Africans offer a dazzling display of daisies from late spring through fall. Being evergreen, they are commonly used as a ground cover, particularly the trailing varieties. A kaleidoscope of colors is available, often with intriguing dark centers bordered by flecks of contrasting color. Several named varieties are available in milder areas of the West, where they are hardy in Zones 9 and 10. Anywhere else, treat them as annuals. Especially attractive to: Most small and mid-size butterflies.

Gooseneck
Lysimachia clethroides

Most lysimachias are yellow-flowered and invasive. This one runs somewhat, but has the most distinctive white flowers. Rising to three feet, the topmost ten inches or so is a narrow cone of tiny flowers, arching gracefully, with the very tip jauntily pointing upward. The flowering stems have the curious habit of all pointing in the same direction, giving the clump the whimsical look of a flock of floral geese. Hardy to Zone 4. Especially attractive to: Swallowtails, Viceroy, and Monarch.

Hollyhock *Alcea rosea*

The stately, old-fashioned single hollyhocks are hard to find on a seed rack — the mania for novelty has left us with nothing but graceless doubles. Worse still are dwarf double hollyhocks, vegetable Munchkins that are the antithesis of everything innately "hollyhock." Perhaps an older friend grows the Real Thing. Cultivate that friendship and acquire some seeds. Goethe grew and loved hollyhocks, and no one has "improved" on *him,* either. Rust on the lower leaves can be a problem; an organic fungicide called Plantvax controls it. Or plant something in front to hide the offending sight. Hardy to Zone 2. Especially attractive to: Painted Lady and West Coast Lady.

Japanese Burnet
Sanguisorba obtusa

Japanese burnet's mound of handsome, toothy, pinnate leaves gives rise to rose-pink bottle-brushes waving about on willowy stems. The effect is charming and whimsical. It appreciates a moist soil, rewarding you with blooms on into the fall. Hardy to Zone 3. Especially attractive to: Milbert's Tortoiseshell, Gray Hairstreak, skippers, and Comma.

Ornamental Onion
Allium spp.

Encompassing dozens of species and varieties, most *Allium* species bear drumstick-clusters of mauvy-pink or purple flowers atop thin stems. Tall types are *A. giganteum* and *A. aflatunense.* Smaller, white-flowered *A. tuberosum,* garlic chives, is also an Oriental herb. Widely available are *A. ostrowskianum* (bright rose-purple), *A. neapolitanum* (white), and *A. moly* (golden yellow). Hardiness varies, but there are some for every climate.

Red Valerian
Centranthus ruber

Not a true valerian, and not even a close look-alike, red valerian is a Eurasian native that has naturalized in North America, particularly California. Capable of growing from out of the tiniest pavement crack or wall chink, it is perhaps best used in rough areas. The two-foot stalks bear elongated clusters of tiny flowers in an odd shade of scarlet-pink, deeper red, or a lovely white. Hardy to Zone 3. Especially attractive to: Gulf Fritillary, Buckeye, Painted Lady, and Milbert's Tortoiseshell.

Sea Holly *Eryngium* spp.

The common name for this plant is rather misleading, since only one species grows near the sea. Most European members of the genus display the same remarkable blueness as *Echinops*. They, too, resemble thistles, or matter. The flowers, while still useful to butterflies, are mostly green curios. It is their foliage that is their glory. With names like *E. agavifolium, E. bromeliifolium,* and *E. yuccifolium,* bold, toothy foliage is the rule. The last one, native to American prairies, bears the intriguing common name of

perhaps teasels, surrounded by a ruff of bracts, often of lacy filigree. They are, however, relatives of parsley. *E. alpinum* is the finest, with *E. amethystinum* a good second. A nice blue form of *E. planum* is also worthwhile, particularly for cutting. The American species are an entirely different "rattlesnake master." Easy to grow from root cuttings or fresh seed, these plants are often self-sowing. But don't waste your time with seed from commercial packets. Good drainage is a must. Most are hardy to Zone 5.

Shasta Daisy

Chrysanthemum × superbum

From six-inch dwarfs to three-foot whoppers, there is a Shasta for every garden. White "petals" surrounding yellow centers create the classic appearance, as in 'Alaska'; 'Marconi' and 'Aglaya' are shaggy and fringed. The longest bloom season occurs in the double-flowered 'Esther Read'. These are all good old dependable varieties, multiplying quickly, and, while lacking the cachet of the latest in trendy unobtainables, are as indispensable and comforting as a favorite pair of slippers. Hardy to Zone 3. Especially attractive to: Milbert's Tortoiseshell, Mourning Cloak, and Red Admiral.

× *Solidaster*

This unusual cross between an aster and a goldenrod produced a two-foot plant with elongated clusters of tiny soft-yellow daisies. As with many hybrids, no viable seed is formed. But in its efforts to do so, the plant continues in bloom for many weeks. The variety 'Lemore' is a most valuable plant. Hardy to Zone 4. Especially attractive to: Viceroy, Comma, Painted Lady, and Silvery Blue.

Tickseed *Coreopsis* spp.

With a common name like that, is it any wonder that "coreopsis" is actually used more often? The most readily available varieties of *C. grandiflora,* such as 'Sunburst', are easily raised from seed, but are not very long-lived. Yet many people find the perky yellow flowers, blooming for months, a must. Just as floriferous, but more soundly perennial, is *C. verticillata.* This delicate-looking, thread-leaved plant colonizes moderately, soon forming sizable patches of airy golden flowers. 'Zagreb' is a deeper gold. Similar of habit is *C. rosea,* with pink flowers. Make sure you get a richly colored form; some types, unfortunately, have all the color intensity of wet Kleenex tissues. Surprisingly, one of these wan forms, it has been surmised, was crossed with *C. verticillata* to produce the very lovely pale-yellow 'Moonlight', often rated as one of the top ten perennials. Hardy to Zone 3. Especially attractive to: Red Admiral, Gray Hairstreak, and Viceroy.

Verbena *Verbena* spp.

V. canadensis is a bone-hardy North American native, eighteen inches tall, and covered with shocking-purple flowers. Hardy to Zone 2. Of similar stature but more tender are varieties of *V. rigida* and *V. tenuisecta,* which bloom all summer and fall. The giant is *V. bonariensis,* whose branched wiry stems support a haze of purple blossoms. Masses of happy orange skippers and Viceroys make for a particularly brilliant sight. Hardy to Zone 7.

The golden flowers of threadleaf tickseed, LEFT, *are a joy for months.*

Yarrow *Achillea* spp.

Ferny-leaved yarrows bear ideal butterfly flowers: flat clusters of little daisies in brilliant hues. *A. millefolium* varieties range from white through intense cerise, and can spread too vigorously underground. The more refined, gray-leaved, pale-yellow-flowered *A. taygetea* and 'Moonshine' stay put; they have been recently crossed with *A. millefollium* so a whole range of interesting shades is now available, descriptively called 'Paprika' and 'Salmon Beauty', to name a few. The tall *A. filipendulina* varieties, such as 'Coronation Gold' and 'Gold Plate', are a difficult-to-integrate shade of mustard. Another clumping species, *A. decolorans,* is represented by its variety 'W. B. Child'. Its airy panicles of half-inch white daisies bloom over a long period and resemble feverfew. Hardy to Zone 3.

Late summer and autumn

Japanese Anemone
Anemone × *hybrida*

Elegant blossoms, in pristine white, dusty rose, or hot pink, perch above handsome grape-looking leaves on this irresistible plant. Each flower is set off by a mint-green button of stamens and angled forward so that it faces you full-on. It prefers some shade and needs enough space so that it won't encroach on less vigorous plants, such as at the edge of a woodland. Hardy to Zone 5.

Aster, Michaelmas Daisy *Aster* spp.

What would an autumn border be without good old Michaelmas daisies, whether the tall varieties, such as 'Harrington's Pink', 'Climax', or 'September Ruby', or the dwarfed versions, such as 'Prof. Kippenburg', 'Opal', or 'Eventide'? From crispest white, through pink and periwinkle, to deepest blue-violet, an entire garden could be made of them. Curiously, the whites are not very appealing to butterflies. Hardy to Zone 2. But if you plant only one perennial aster, make it *Aster* × *frikartii*. Three-foot mounds of gray-green foliage set off the one-and-a-half-inch gold-centered lavender daisies. Hardy to Zone 5.

Border Sages *Salvia* spp.

The autumn-blooming salvias tend to be a fairly tender lot, but many are easily overwintered indoors, and are so fast-growing that rooted cuttings rapidly produce full-size plants. Among the best for your butterfly garden are *S. guaranitica,* growing to five feet, with royal-blue flowers; *S. azurea* (a.k.a. *S. pitcheri*), whose sky-blue flowers are gorgeous with the Michaelmas daisy 'Harrington's Pink'; and *S. leucantha,* with two-foot wands of white tubular flowers subtended by persistent bright-purple fuzzy calyxes, producing quite a show in September. Perennial in Zones 7–10. Especially attractive to: Monarch, Viceroy, swallowtails, and Great Spangled Fritillary.

Wild white yarrow, ABOVE, *will take over your garden, but many tractable forms of this butterfly favorite exist from which to choose.*

Coneflower *Rudbeckia* spp.

The signature flower of the dog-days, coneflower's gold and mahogany tones manage to look rousing in even the most stultifying heat. Popular varieties are *R. fulgida* 'Goldsturm', and the seven-foot *R.* *nitida* 'Herbstsonne' ('Autumn Sun'), whose single yellow daisies are set off by lime gumdrop centers. Hardy to Zone 2. Especially attractive to: Silvery Blue, Great Spangled Fritillary, Monarch, swallowtails, and Viceroy.

Joe-Pye Weed

Eupatorium purpureum

Looking for all the world like a large-scale ageratum, the native *E. purpureum* usually tops out at four feet. Hardy to Zone 4. Especially attractive to: Painted Lady, Great Spangled Fritillary, Monarch, and swallowtails.

Purple Coneflower

Echinacea purpurea

A flower enjoying a revival in the herb garden, purple coneflower's three-foot stems support three-inch daisies of dusty mauve to near white, centered with a boss of rusty ochre — an unusual combination of colors. A sturdy prairie native, it is hardy to Zone 3. Especially attractive to: Great Spangled Fritillary, Viceroy, and Tawny-edged Skipper.

Stonecrop *Sedum* spp.

These succulents produce some of the best butterfly flowers in the garden. Tops is 'Autumn Joy', whose flat clusters of bright-mauve flowers age to a subtle shade of brick. The stalks persist into winter, bleached to buff and biscuit. Hardy to Zone 3. Especially attractive to: Comma, Milbert's Tortoise-shell, Painted Lady, and Red Admiral.

A Silver-spotted Skipper feeds on the tiny florets of the "cone" of the purple coneflower, BELOW.

ANNUALS AND BIENNIALS

Because annuals and biennials complete their entire life cycle in such a short time, the urge to reproduce means that they tend to bloom extravagantly. Plants that flower so profusely are bound to be well loved and widely grown. Whereas many perennials and shrubs are known by their scientific names, most annuals are known by common names, as a testament to the affection we feel for them. They will grow in all zones.

The Top Ten

Ageratum, Flossflower
Ageratum houstonianum

Blooming in mid- to late summer, ageratum sports fluffy heads of blue or white. It grows to one foot high. Especially attractive to: Milbert's Tortoiseshell and Red Admiral.

Cosmos *Cosmos* hybrids

These well-known flowers last all summer, until frost. Smaller-flowered orange and scarlet varieties reach thirty inches, while robust pink varieties reach five feet.

Globe candytuft
Iberis umbellata

Globe candytuft graces the garden from late spring through summer. It is often included in scatter-garden mixes. Though similar to the perennial species, these come in a range of colors from carmine through pink, lavender, and white. The plant will self-sow with a little encouragement. Especially attractive to: White Admiral, Silvery Blue, and Spring Azure.

Bespangled with jewels, a Black Swallowtail alights on a raspberry pink cosmos, BELOW.

Heliotrope, Cherry-Pie Plant
Heliotropium arborescens

Summer through fall, heliotrope offers a garden display. The intense fragrance of intermingled vanilla and almond gave rise to the second, evocative common name. Some newer hybrids have deep-purple coloring but little fragrance. The older, paler forms are the sweetest. Actually a tender perennial, a superior plant can be overwintered and started from cuttings. This is a most enticing flower for the butterflies in your garden.

Lantana *Lantana* hybrids

Blooming spring through fall, and year-round in frost-free areas, lantana is a tender plant, and also one of the best attractants. Flowers are either scarlet and yellow, or lavender. It looks especially wonderful hanging or draped over a wall. Especially attractive to: Gulf Fritillary, Monarch, Spicebush Swallowtail, and Cabbage White.

Marigold *Tagetes* hybrids

A garden favorite, marigold blooms summer through fall. Many heights and sizes of flowers are available, in colors ranging from primrose through gold, orange, and mahogany-red. Especially attractive to: Milbert's Tortoiseshell and West Coast Lady.

Mexican Sunflower, Torch Flower
Tithonia rotundifolia

The commanding, eight-foot-tall torch flower has rounded, daisylike flowers in a subtle shade of orange. They attract a constant cloud of hovering butterflies from late summer through fall. The scene is particularly striking when dozens of Monarchs flit about.

Nasturtium
Tropaeolum hybrids

Both the dwarf edging types and the trailing or climbing types of nasturtiums furnish a banquet for butterflies, in nectar and as a larval food source. Profuse flowers of yellow, scarlet, and cherry-red, often with darker penciling, bloom from summer through fall. Especially attractive to: Cabbage White, Painted Lady, and White Admiral.

Lantana, LEFT, *blooms virtually year-round in mild climates. In harsher climes, it makes a wonderful summer show.*

Zinnia *Zinnia* hybrids

There are many varieties of zinnia — from dwarf buttons to tall shaggy cactus-flowers — and they range in color from jewel tones of scarlet, ruby, and cerise to orange, gold, primrose, creamy white, and even ice green. At their finest from summer to fall, the season when so many things flag, they give so much for so little. Especially attractive to: Painted Lady, White Admiral, and West Coast Lady.

Sweet Alyssum
Lobularia maritima

Tiny, honey-scented flowers clothe small edging plants from spring through fall, attracting myriad smaller butterflies. The standard white form has been augmented by rose and midnight purple. Especially attractive to: Cabbage White, Spring Azure, Silvery Blue, Common Sulphur, and skippers.

Other Good Butterfly Annuals

Annual Pinks (*Dianthus chinensis*)
Common Mignonette (*Reseda odorata*)
Forget-Me-Not (*Myosotis* hybrids)
Johnny-Jump-Up (*Viola tricolor*)
Lupine (*Lupinus* spp.)
Mallow (*Lavatera trimestris*)
Petunia (*Petunia* hybrids)
Phlox (*Phlox drummondi*)
Pincushions (*Scabiosa atropurpurea*)
Sunflower (*Helianthus annuus*)
Sweet William (*Dianthus barbatus*)
Verbena (*Verbena* hybrids)

Marigolds, ABOVE, *are great favorites of both butterflies and children. The yellow disc flowers of this zinnia make a brilliant contrast to its "petals,"* LEFT.

VINES

A few vines play indispensable roles in the life cycles of certain butterflies, mostly as larval food sources. If the corresponding butterflies are native to your area, planting these vines is sure to lure them to your garden.

Common Hops

Humulus lupulus

These vigorous vines die to the ground each winter, so they never build up a great tangled mass. In late summer, clusters of pale celadon flowers, like small papery pine cones, festoon the vines, and are used in brewing. A golden-leaved version, 'Aureus', is extremely ornamental. Hardy to Zone 4. Especially attractive to: Red Admiral, Comma, and Gray Hairstreak.

Dutchman's Pipe

Aristolochia spp.

Several native species of *Aristolochia* will do in furnishing food for the caterpillars of the Pipevine Swallowtail. All have curious dangling, swollen, and recurved flowers that look for all the world like old-fashioned tobacco pipes. The large, heart-shaped leaves are tropical-looking. Hardy to Zone 5.

Honeysuckle *Lonicera* spp.

The white- and yellow-flowered species are more sweetly scented. The red and orange ones are bird flowers, and therefore unscented. All possess nectar, the scented ones being more attractive to butterflies. Hardy in Zones 4 – 10. Especially attractive to: Spicebush Swallowtail.

Sweet Pea *Lathyrus odoratus*

This favorite annual vine needs no introduction. The 'Royal Family' strain is the most heat-resistant. Flower production decreases drastically if seeds are allowed to set, so pick the flowers every other day. Hardy in all zones. Especially attractive to: Silvery Blue.

Passionflower

Passiflora spp.

Beautiful foliage, lobed like a small fig leaf, sets off these most unusual flowers, the components of which suggested episodes in Christ's passion to some bygone pious observer. The egg-shaped fruit is both decorative and edible. Caterpillars of the Gulf Fritillary call this vine home. Hardy from Zones 1 through 10 (varies with species).

The striking passionflower, OPPOSITE, *grows on a vine and is as ornamental as it is useful for attracting butterflies.*

HERBS

Since most herbs prefer the same open, sunny conditions that attract butterflies, and since the great majority of them are wonderful nectar sources, try incorporating some herbs into your design. Many herbs have extra-ornamental forms, such as bronze fennel, purple or variegated sage, golden or variegated marjoram, mint, and lemon balm, and the many kinds of thyme. And don't confine herbs to formal herb gardens. They can provide crevice plants for walls and crazy paving, accent plants, and, as many of them have gray fuzzy leaves, act as a textural as well as visual contrast to more typical ornamentals. Since their foliage looks good all season, herbs can furnish the required "good bones" for a mixed planting.

MOTH FLOWERS

Night-scented, trumpet-shaped flowers lure these ethereal creatures. The nocturnal flutterings of moths, rendered even more mysterious by the darkness, create an otherworldly atmosphere. Your garden becomes a completely different environment from the sparkling gem of the sunny daytime.

Four-O'Clock

Mirabilis jalapa

The name of this semi-hardy perennial, which can be treated as an annual, refers to the time of day when the two-inch trumpet-shaped flowers open. They bloom for many weeks in shades of red, white, yellow, and striped combinations of these colors. Hardy in zones 7 through 10.

Flowering Tobacco

Nicotiana hybrids

Often called by its botanical name, *Nicotiana,* flowering tobacco's trumpet flowers can be colored crimson, pink, white, and lime green. The newer dwarf strains make floriferous garden plants, but aren't nearly as fragrant (or, therefore, as attractive to moths) as the taller, older strains, which bloom in more subtle mauve and lavender tones. *N. alata* 'Grandiflora' is the species behind all of these varieties, and, if it can be found, is the best form for our purposes. Also, the seven-foot annual *N. sylvestris* bears a mass of nocturnally fragrant white flowers. The tube of each blossom is three inches long, and very narrow. The flowers droop gracefully from the top of the plant, creating a dramatic but graceful accent in late summer.

Moonflower

Calonyction aculeatum

A perennial vine, moonflower is grown as an annual in the North and is related to morning glory. The sweetly scented five-inch white or pale-pink flowers open after nightfall and last until the following morning. They will grow to ten feet or more, and are ideal for training up a porch trellis or over a summerhouse. Will grow in all zones, but need warmth to thrive.

Night-Scented Jasmine

Cestrum nocturnum

A shrub featuring heavy clusters of one-inch tubular green flowers in summer, night-scented jasmine's fragrance is cloyingly sweet up close, but ravishingly tropical from a distance. Hardy in Zone 9, worth a try in warm-summer areas of Zone 8.

Many herbs, like this catmint, LEFT, *are both highly attractive to butterflies and of easy culture — requiring ordinary soil and moderate watering.*

BIRD FLOWERS

In North America, the various species of hummingbirds are the nectar-seekers that will visit your garden. Hovering as they probe each flower, or flashing brilliantly in a territorial or mating display, they are more than welcome in our gardens.

East of the Rockies, the only hummingbird is the Rubythroat. In the West, there are numerous species, some resident year-round as far north as Vancouver Island, as long as winter food supplies last. Hummingbird feeders, filled with sugar syrup, can ensure that winter holdouts have enough nourishment to survive until spring. Planting bird flowers in your garden will guarantee these creatures' antics in the summer.

Bird flowers tend to be tubular; some shades of red, orange, or purple; and scentless. They are often borne on spires above the foliage to allow easy access.

Herbaceous Bird Flowers

Bee Balm (*Monarda* spp.)
California Fuchsia (*Zauschneria* spp.)
Columbine (*Aquilegia* spp., particularly *A. formosa* and *A. canadensis*)
Coralbells (*Heuchera sanguinea* vars.)
Cypress Vine (*Ipomoea quamoclit*)

Foxglove (*Digitalis* spp.)
Obedient Plant (*Physostegia* vars.)
Poker Flower (*Kniphofia* spp.)
Sage (*Salvia elegans, S. greggii,* etc.)
Snapdragon (*Antirrhinum* vars.)

Woody Bird Flowers

Abelia (*Abelia* spp.)
Chilean Flame Tree (*Embothrium coccineum*)
Escallonia (*Escallonia* vars.)
Flowering Currant (*Ribes sanguineum*)
Flowering Maple (*Abutilon* spp.)
Fuchsia (*Fuchsia* vars.)

Honeysuckle, particularly the red-flowered ones (*Lonicera* spp.)
New Zealand Christmas Tree (*Metrosideros excelsus*)
Phygelius (*Phygelius capensis*)
Trumpet Vine (*Campsis radicans*)
Weigela (*Weigela* vars.)

This casual mixture of flowers at the edge of a wood, LEFT, *is ideal for luring both butterflies and hummingbirds.*

FIVE

DESIGNING A MAGNIFICENT BUTTERFLY GARDEN

It's all well and good to plan your

garden with the theme of attracting

and accommodating butterflies, but

it needn't be an approximation of

the wilderness. Within this chapter,

you will tour different butterfly

gardens, each with its own design

geared both to the locale and the specific tastes of its creators.

The first section, "The Public Butterfly Garden," will acquaint you with the numerous possibilities for creating ultimate butterfly environments. While most gardeners simply do not have the facilities to support such specialized features as glass-enclosed conservatories, they can incorporate elements of these environments — such as offering butterfly "treats" in birdbaths — to their own garden schemes.

The next section, "The Personal Butterfly Garden," presents two specialized designs created especially with the butterfly in mind. Though you need not follow these plans to the letter, you are certain to learn from them and derive ideas for your own yard. Even if you only have room for just a scattering of butterfly bushes, zinnias, and marigolds, you will certainly come to know the butterfly's habits more intimately by examining and enjoying the gardens presented here.

The appropriately named butterfly bush perfumes the air, coaxing butterflies from near and far, ABOVE.

The Public Butterfly Garden

Anyone with at least a moderate interest in butterflies and butterfly gardening will take pleasure in visiting one of the many public butterfly gardens that have been created, both in the United States and abroad. I first heard of such places while traveling in Britain, where several of the large estates that are open to the public maintain special environments for butterflies.

No less a figure than Sir Winston Churchill is largely responsible for popularizing butterflies as a feature on the grounds of stately homes. For years at Chartwell, his home in Kent, Churchill maintained a garden for the benefit of more than a thousand butterflies, and he stocked it yearly. To get the most enjoyment out of the situation, he converted a summerhouse to a caterpillar and chrysalis shelter, where the many exotic butterflies found in the garden could enjoy a controlled environment that encouraged reproduction and metamorphosis.

The public butterfly garden is a very new idea in North America. It is only since the late 1980s that any facilities approaching the scale of the London Butterfly House have opened on this side of the Atlantic. Now, from Coconut Creek, Florida, to the Bay Area of California, public butterfly gardens are either open or in the planning stages. Foremost among them is the one within Callaway Gardens, near Pine Mountain, Georgia, in the Appalachians. Devoted to the nurturing and enjoyment of butterflies, the garden features the Cecil B. Day Butterfly Center, the largest glass-enclosed free-flight conservatory in North America.

Butterfly gardens usually have a repertoire of novel techniques to attract residents. Special treats, such as overripe bananas and sugar syrup, are often proffered. Callaway Gardens devised a particularly clever method of feeding butterflies. Since these creatures can't drink directly from a pool of liquid, bright-orange scrubbers are added to sugar-syrup-filled birdbaths. The scrubbers wick up the liquid while also attracting butterflies with their appealing color.

Because they recreate specialized environments, such as that of the tropical rain forest, public butterfly gardens present unparalleled opportunities to observe unusual species. *Ixora, Pentas,* palms, lianas, and other tropical plants, combined with proper temperature conditions, make it possible for extravagantly patterned exotic butterflies to thrive. In such an environment, the visitor will observe tropical species with bold zebra stripes of gold and black, or orange and black stripes; electric-blue markings; scarlet patches; and silver streaks. These environments also support some of nature's finest examples of mimicry, such as the appropriately named dead-leaf butterflies. Perched on plants, these butterflies appear to be brown leaves, camouflaging them from predators.

Butterfly gardens also afford their visitors a rare display of tropical-species chrysalises (a chrysalis is the intermediate resting stage between caterpillar and butterfly). Just as tropical butterflies are more showy than are North American natives, so are their chrysalises. Although some are a low-key mahogany and russet, often with protuberances to further create the illusion of dead twigs and leaves, many are positively flamboyant. Acid-green, golden-yellow, and brilliant-metallic shades are common chrysalis colors that can be observed from close up in these sanctuaries.

The Cecil B. Day Butterfly Center at Callaway Gardens, Georgia, ABOVE, *is a dazzling living display of both well-known and exotic species.*

The Personal Butterfly Garden

A butterfly garden must appeal to *your* sense of beauty, first and foremost. Fortunately, there are many plants that are highly ornamental, appropriate to traditional garden styles, and that just happen to attract butterflies as well. By including these, you will create an environment that is both pleasing to you, and suited to your winged guests.

Before you plunge ahead with choosing the flowers for your garden, there are some further considerations you must keep in mind in terms of butterfly appeal. Butterflies are creatures of the sun, unable to produce their own body heat. Not only are they inactive below temperatures around 50 degrees Fahrenheit, but they need the sun for navigation, as described in Chapter 2. Therefore, a heavily shaded garden or one on the north side of a house will not prove very inviting. A southern exposure is ideal, but east or west are acceptable. The image you should have in mind is that of a sunny meadow at the edge of the woods. The flowers of the open area furnish nectar, while the trees provide shelter and protection, as well as food for larvae. Bear in mind that trees casting light shade, such as mimosa or honey locust, are preferable to beeches and the larger maples, particularly if you have limited garden space.

Butterfly wings are delicate things, prone to tearing in strong or gusty wind. A sheltered garden site is therefore important. The air needn't be dead-still, but the strong winds of coastal or mountain areas need modifying. Fences and walls seem the obvious choices, but, in reality, solid barriers can cause more problems than they solve. Wind rushing over the top of such structures creates chaotic eddies and swirls on the lee side that can be more troublesome than a steady prevailing wind. A louvered or lattice fence festooned with vines will baffle the wind, reducing its impact greatly. Hedges are even better, since they can be composed of butterfly plants. Think beyond privet and boxwood and their clipped formality. Lilacs, firethorn, mock orange, ceanothus, viburnum, cotoneasters, osmanthus, and butterfly bush are all good choices for a more informal look, and butterflies like them all, too. Plus, they're much less work than a formal hedge, and usually require only a yearly going-over.

Still another reason for incorporating shrubs and trees in your garden is for nighttime protection of your butterflies. Like birds, butterflies roost in the shelter of trees and shrubs. There, safe from predators, they rest with their wings folded, revealing only the camouflaged undersides.

Borders of herbaceous perennials are glorious, but it's probably more advisable for your purposes to mix things up a bit. Many perennials have but a two-week bloom period, and too many such ephemerals, with different peak periods, together in a border can create a spotty hodgepodge. A few smaller shrubs intermixed can add much in texture and form, as well as contributing their flowers. Foliage plants, such as hostas, rodgersias, ornamental grasses, and silvery artemisias, furnish the season-long "bones" of the garden, around which more floriferous plants come and go in their time.

Don't overlook annuals. Many bloom in prodigal abundance, throughout the whole of summer and into the fall. Several among them are classic butterfly plants. Ageratum, sweet alyssum, cosmos, verbena, and the pincushion flower are real champions when it comes to ease of culture and duration of bloom. They are best planted in groups, not only because such drifts of flowers are more aesthetically pleasing to our human senses, but also because a significant

number of flowers of one type, blooming in a mass, holds a greater attraction for butterflies than do single plants, or plants in single-file rows.

Bear in mind the necessity of "deadheading" most annuals. Since it is their mission in life to produce seed for the next year, they will cease blooming if allowed to set seed. Assiduous removal of spent blossoms may not be the greatest pleasure you take in your garden, but the constant encouragement derived from the butterflies dancing about you as you pinch away should alleviate some of the drudgery.

If you choose to have an area of lawn in your garden, you'll be pleased to know that you now have a reason to allow a few weeds to remain. English daisies, speedwell, clover, and even dandelions are all sought out by butterflies. A greensward spangled with flowers is a charming sight; certainly more so than the self-conscious perfection of a putting green. Clipping the grass to two inches will allow these delightful interlopers to thrive. Besides, grass is healthier when it's not cropped too severely.

Aside from nectar sources, butterflies need an occasional drink of water, and your garden should provide for this. In fact, small flocks of swallowtails, skippers, blues, and

Two tropical butterflies show their glorious colors and markings in a butterfly house, ABOVE. *It takes a long proboscis to get at the nectar in a long-tubed flower, as shown at right.*

sulphurs often gather together to form "drinking clubs." But as butterflies cannot drink from open water, a birdbath-type facility won't work, unless you adapt a technique similar to the one at Callaway. What is needed is a sunny damp spot, be it sandy or muddy. A small plastic basin, buried in the soil and filled with sand or earth, will furnish just the right amount of moisture. If you put the basin near a hose bibb, it will be easier for you to keep it filled. Placing a few rocks near-by affords butterfly perching spots.

The basic formula, then, is to plant taller trees and shrubs at the perimeter of the garden (particularly on the windy side), with shorter shrubs and herbaceous plants in front of them. A central area of lawn or some sort of pavement will not only allow for a feeling of openness, which butterflies need, but will also create a wonderful vantage point for you to sit on a summer day, lemonade in hand, watching the aerial ballet all about you.

Two Designs

No matter where you live, short of the Arctic Circle, it is possible to have a garden that both you and your butterfly guests will enjoy. Regional conditions of climate, geology, and architectural heritage exert varying degrees of influence on just what style of garden you design. The rocky soils of New England and the Maritimes often mean stone walls and outcrops, which would look artificial on the sandy flatlands of Florida or the plains of Nebraska. Pavement or native grasses for the open spaces of an Arizona garden are far more appropriate than a sweep of classic bluegrass turf.

Equally inappropriate is a garden style that has nothing to do with its resident buildings. A sleek, angular modern home, with vast areas of glass, would look silly surrounded by a fidgety cottage garden. Likewise, a gingerbread-laden Victorian is not conducive to the serenity of the Japanese-garden style.

Whatever style your home and native surroundings are, it is possible to adapt the principles of butterfly gardening to your landscape. Beds of just one kind of flower, usually an annual, carry out the picture begun by a modern home of large, uncluttered line and shape, while herbaceous or shrub borders suit a more highly ornamented structure. A strong sense of spatial organization, or "good bones," is vital in any garden. The plants may tumble out from the confines of their beds with seeming abandon, but without a clear underlying organization, a garden can degenerate into chaos.

The garden designs that follow are ideal spaces created expressly for butterfly lovers. They are based on standard garden-design principles, with special attention to the requirements of butterflies. For instance, the division of the spaces, their relations to one another, and the sight lines or garden views all follow tried and true rules. However, the special needs of butterflies for shelter and sunny open space, as well as lots of flowers, influence both the arrangement of space and the kinds of plants used in the gardens. In general, where any of several types of plants would suit a generic design, the plant most favored by butterflies is chosen.

Portions of these gardens, with adaptation, are suitable for just about any region or architectural style. Pick

FIGURE 1

and choose the elements that appeal most to you, and use the plant lists found in this book to design your own garden, one that reflects your personal taste. Perhaps it won't be Giverny or Sissinghurst, but it will be beautiful, it will be yours, and it will be full of butterflies!

The garden illustrated in Figure 1 is actually composed of many gardens — each with its own design features, and each fulfilling a unique purpose. Overall, the garden measures 144 feet by 112 feet, and its plantings were chosen not only on the basis of beauty, but also because of their ability to endure cold (they are hardy to Zone 4, which is quite northerly).

For the sake of convenience, each component garden can be considered an outdoor "room." Just as an indoor room may have polished hardwood floors and Oriental rugs, or wall-to-wall carpet, outdoors, the "floor" can be of pavement (concrete, brick, or flagstone) or grass. Plants, and their arrangement, make up the furnishings of a garden room. As with the interior of a home, the rooms of a garden must be organized logically.

The rooms in Figure 1 flow from the terrace (1), to a large, public sweep of lawn leading to a private summerhouse (9) and a delightful bosky area at the rear of the garden. A vine-covered latticework fence (20) separates the open lawn from a traditional herbaceous border (16), brightened with beds of annuals (19). The main axis of this room (18) takes the garden visitor back to the fragrant rose garden (21).

Separating the terrace from the open lawn area is a single row of columns, surmounted by a simple trellis structure of beam and cross members. This structure not only defines the terrace, but frames the vista to the wooded end of the garden, while also furnishing a support for butterfly-loving vines such as common hops, purple wisteria, and sweet pea. Since the terrace is likely to be used in the evening, the beds beneath the columns are planted with white flowers, which show up in reduced light. Also, such moth flowers as four-o'clocks and fragrant nicotiana are planted here. The six-foot *Nicotiana*

sylvestris would be an excellent choice in accent clumps.

Looking into the garden, you'll notice that the lawn area is not a perfect rectangle. A "peninsula" with a clump of birches (5) divides the space nearly in half. These trees attract an array of beautiful species. Nearby the birches, a border of shrubs (4) fronts a row of Amur maples (3). The shrubs include various viburnums, fragrant mock orange (*Philadelphus* spp.), varieties of bush cinquefoil (*Potentilla fruticosa*) for all-summer bloom, spireas, and the late-summer sweetness of sweet pepperbush (*Clethra* spp.) and bluebeard (*Caryopteris* spp.). An 'Idaho' locust tree shades the rear of the area, its hanging clusters of rosy bloom scenting the June air. All these trees and shrubs provide screening from the neighbors, as well as wind protection for your butterflies. Aside from these plants producing some of the best butterfly flowers of spring and summer, year-round interest is created by the brilliant maples of autumn and the stark white of the birches in winter.

The summerhouse is perched atop a small rise, with a wide flight of steps making a gracious transition from garden to resting spot. The side of this slope is shored up with a rough stone wall (8), with plenty of crannies left for wall plants. Rock cress, aubrieta, and creeping phlox, plus hardy sedums, are good butterfly plants to tuck into the chinks. Near the base of the end of this wall would be an ideal place for a "butterfly puddle," a sunny, open spot with ample perching spots nearby.

The summerhouse itself is a simple, rustic structure, perhaps made of weathered, peeled branches and small logs. Planted at the base, and clambering over the top, is a trumpet vine (*Campsis* spp.) with striking coral blossoms, a proven favorite of hummingbirds. Behind the summerhouse, for additional screening, are native pussy willows (7), a favorite food of many caterpillars. The margins of this secluded spot are planted with a lilac or two, bush cinquefoil, bluebeard, and other easy-care shrubs of smaller scale. An *Amelanchier laevis* (10) provides early butterflies with nectar from its masses of white blossoms, feeds birds with the blue-black berries that follow, and, later, delights you with its brilliant fall foliage. That such a small tree should be decorated with so many common names—shadblow, serviceberry (or sarvis berry), June berry, and snowy mespilus among them—is witness to its popularity.

The amelanchier also marks the transition to a wooded area of loftier trees (12). Here, hornbeams, hackberries, cottonwoods, elms, and maples

are appropriate, furnishing caterpillar food and overnight roosting sites for adults. The area between the tall woods and the flat lawn (11) is planted with viburnums (*Viburnum dentatum* and *V. prunifolium*), and similar butterfly-attracting taller "woodsy" shrubs. This area of intermediate height is also important to the birds in your garden. Many shier species need this shrubby area of medium height from which to venture forth into the open.

A pair of small trees marks the boundary between "civilized" and "wild" areas of the garden. A plum (13) is favored by spring butterflies and fruit-feasting summer birds, while a hawthorn (14) contributes nectar, leaves for caterpillars, and scarlet winter berries for you and the birds.

The herbaceous border area (16) not only has the greatest concentration of flowers, but is also the most wind-protected spot in the garden, making it the most likely location for butterfly-viewing. Screening is provided by a lattice fence, planted with butterfly vines and a row of various kinds of lilac species and hybrids, including the graceful Prestoniae hybrids. Helping to balance the tall trees at the opposite end, a Russian olive (*Elaeagnus angustifolia*) offers shade and a roosting site amid its silvery leaves. The central lawn (18) creates the open space butterflies prefer, while a mixture of perennials and shrubs on one side, and beds of annuals on the other supply an abundance of nectar.

Colors are arranged after the manner of that great color theorist of the garden, Gertrude Jekyll, with tones of pink and rose, pale yellow and blue, harmonizing with one another. At the rear of the border is a narrow path that disappears between the lilacs and tall perennials — a must for access to the area's nether regions.

The gemlike rose garden is planted with a variety of fragrant species — miniature roses, old-fashioned varieties, ramblers, and climbers, which scramble up a trellis — and is sure to attract a number of butterflies, such as the striped hairstreaks in caterpillar stage, which favor rose family members as host plants. There is also an underplanting of thymes, cat mints, sedums, heliotrope, and creeping phlox — all butterfly attractants.

Perhaps you don't have the space for such a substantial garden, but any of these design ideas can be adapted to a smaller space. For those who have an average-size lot, the garden illustrated in Figure 2 may be even more intriguing. This plan is modeled after the richly varied yet diminutive plots typically found in California, a climate that favors Mediterranean plantings

because of its lower summer rainfall and lack of humidity. But even for those who don't live in such an environment, plenty can be learned here, and substitution plants are suggested.

A lovely selection of trees and shrubs is an essential feature of this garden — not only for their impressive butterfly-attractant qualities, but also for the shade, sense of depth, and beauty they contribute to the space. They also afford privacy for people *and* protection for gossamer butterfly wings. Included in the arc formation around the perimeter are chinese dogwoods (*Cornus kousa* var. *chinensis*), a 'Bleiriana' flowering plum, and a Washington hawthorn (*Crataegus phaenopyrum*). The Chinese dogwood selected here is suitable for planting anywhere in the country and is covered with starry white flowers that turn from pink to wine red as summer progresses. One of the first trees to flower in spring, the plum furnishes food for butterflies as early as February. For extra color, vining golden hops is planted at the base of the plum, where it can hoist itself up and over. Many species of butterfly feed on hops; this one, *Humulus lupulus* 'Aureus,' has glowing chartreuse foliage guaranteed to light up the plum. All it requires in the way of care is annual removal of the trailing shoots, which die to the ground in the fall. Lastly, the white-flowered hawthorn is a good source of butterfly and caterpillar food, and the scarlet berries last well into the winter, eventually to be eaten by roving bands of robins and waxwings.

The large, central lawn area creates a sunny space for butterflies and people, while the surrounding shrubs and herbaceous plants offer a wealth of fragrant blossom. Shading the patio is a crape myrtle (*Lagerstroemia indica*), which, even if shy to flower in the cool Northwest, charms with its amazingly smooth and sensual pale trunk. (One of its Chinese names means "tree too smooth for monkeys to climb.") Underneath, a carpet of the scented-leaved hardy geranium (*Geranium macrorhizum*) thrives, and this ground cover can also be found at the foot of the line of Mexican oranges (*Choisya ternata*) against the fence. Around the corner of the house, a passionflower (*Passiflora* spp.) vine clothes the fence, luring Gulf Fritillaries from all over.

The patio is separated from the shrub border by a row of hebes (*Hebe* spp.), neat little butterfly-attractant shrubs. In the Southeast, *Pittosporum tobira* 'Wheeler's Dwarf' would be an effective substitute.

Against the fence, butterfly-luring firethorn (*Pyracantha* spp.) displays its creamy blossoms followed by orange or red berries, set off by dark evergreen leaves. A delicate-textured vine from Chile, glory flower (*Eccremocarpus scaber*) twines through, its tubular scarlet, yellow, or rosy-salmon flowers an invitation to passing hummingbirds. Of a larger scale, the shrubby Cape fuchsia (*Phygelius capensis*) or one of its hybrids winds through the firethorn. Its dangling scarlet, salmon, or pale yellow trumpets are equally tempting to the tiny feathered jewels. In front, scented pale-lilac abelia, periwinkle-blue bluebeard (*Caryopteris* spp.), and the shrubby *Potentilla* 'Sutter's Gold' entice butterflies. One of the many crepe-flowered rockroses (*Cistus* spp.) creates a point of solidity in the border, for which viburnum (*Viburnum davidii*), with its quilted leaves and blue berries, could be substituted. At its feet, a California fuchsia (*Zauschneria* spp.) blooms with scarlet, white, or peach bird flowers.

One of the many varieties of butterfly bush (*Buddleia davidii*) fills the space between the hawthorn and the fence, while the hanging carmine clusters of the flowering currant (*Ribes sanguineum*) welcome spring's first returning hummingbirds. Either *R. odoratum* or *R. aureum* would do the job of this western woodlander elsewhere.

Under the trees, woodsy plants hold sway. Tall foxgloves and jaunty colum-

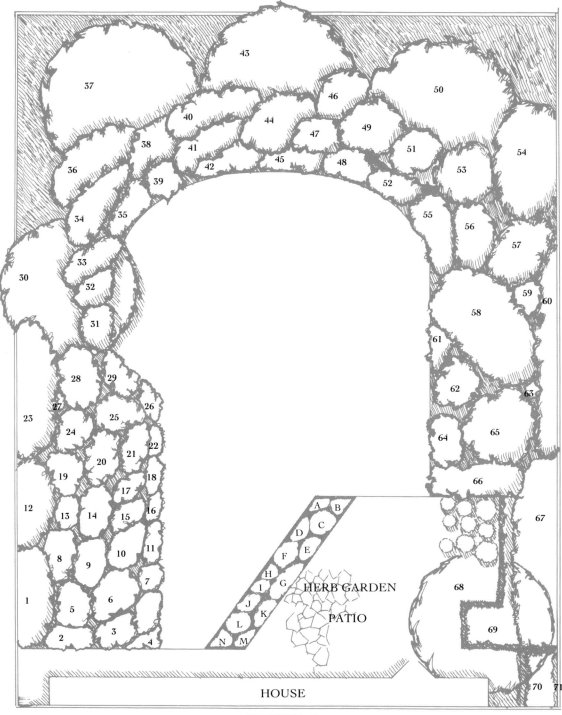

FIGURE 2

1. *Clethra alnifolia* 'Rosea'
2. *Salvia* 'Ost Friesland'
3. *Achillea* 'Moonshine'
4. *Dianthus* × *allwoodii*
5. *Potentilla fruticosa* 'Mt. Everest'
6. *Lysimachia clethroides*
7. *Coreopsis rosea*
8. *Aster* 'Harrington's Pink'
9. *Campanula lactiflora*
10. *Penstemon* 'Evelyn'
11. *Campanula carpatica* 'Blue Clips'
12. *Viburnum carlesii*
13. *Salvia pitcheri*
14. *Phlox* 'Mt. Fuji'
15. *Coreopsis* 'Moonbeams'
16. *Jasione perennis*
17. *Erigeron* 'Darkest of All'
18. *Dianthus* 'Mrs. Sinkins'
19. *Delphinium* 'Blue Jay'
20. *Aster* × *frikartii*
21. *Achillea taygetea*
22. *Heucherella* 'Bridget Bloom'
23. *Viburnum tinus robustus*
24. *Cephalaria gigantea*
25. *Scabiosa caucasica*

26. *Iberis sempervirens*
27. *Clematis viticella*
28. *Verbena bonariensis*
29. *Anthemis* 'Wargrave'
30. *Cornus kousa chinensis* (tree)
31. hosta
32. impatiens
33. *Pulmonaria* 'Mrs. Moon'
34. ferns
35. hardy fuchsia
36. Japanese anemone
37. *Sorbus hupehensis* 'Pink Pagoda' (tree)
38. *Astilbe* 'Ostrich Plume'
39. hosta
40. Japanese anemone
41. *Polemonium caeruleum*
42. impatiens
43. *Prunus* 'Blireiana', golden hops (tree)
44. *Astilbe* 'Deutschland'
45. *Erigeron karvinskianus*
46. ferns
47. columbine
48. hosta

49. foxgloves
50. *Crataegus phaenopyrum* (tree)
51. ferns
52. impatiens
53. *Ribes sanguineum*
54. *Buddleia* 'Dark Knight'
55. *Spirea* 'Little Princess'
56. *Romneya coulteri* 'Butterfly'
57. *Ceanothus* 'Julia Phelps'
58. *Cistus ladanifer* 'Maculatus'
59. *Phygelius* 'Salmon Leap'
60. Pyracantha
61. *Zauschneria* 'Solidarity Pink'
62. *Caryopteris* × *clandonensis*
63. *Eccremocarpus scaber* (pink form)
64. *Potentilla fruticosa* 'Sutter's Gold'
65. *Abelia* × *grandiflora*
66. *Hebe salicifolia*
67. *Choisya ternata*
68. crape myrtle (tree)
69. *Geranium macrorrhizum*
70. *Vinca minor*
71. passion vine

A. *Sedum* 'Vera Jameson'
B. *Antennaria dioica* 'Rosea' (pink pussy toes)
C. *Helictotrichon sempervirens* (evergreen oatgrass)
D. *Salvia officinalis* 'Purpurascens' (purple sage)
E. *Origanum vulgare* 'Aurea' (golden marjoram)

F. *Origanum* 'Hopley's Purple'
G. *Lavandula* 'Munstead' (lavender)
H. *Allium schoenoprasum* 'Forescate'
I. *Origanum vulgare* 'Variegatum' (variegated marjoram)

J. *Ruta graveolens* 'Jackman's Blue' (rue)
K. *Thymus pseudolanuginosus* (woolly thyme)
L. *Salvia officinalis* 'Icterina'
M. *Armeria maritima*
N. *Thymus vulgaris* 'Argentea' (silver thyme)

bine beckon to hummingbirds, while astilbes, Japanese anemones, and Jacob's ladder bloom for weeks amid lacy ferns. Creamy variegated hostas create sparkling pools in the shade, with Mexican daisies (*Erigeron karvinskyanus*) and repeated groupings of impatiens between them, edging the lawn. A hardy fuchsia — a wonderful bird flower — and the silver-spangled leaves of the china-blue winter-flowering lungwort (*Pulmonaria* spp.) complete the scene.

Emerging again into the sun, the border takes on a more traditional herbaceous aspect. Here, backed by the winter-flowering viburnum (*Viburnum*

Overwintering Monarchs gorge themselves on pride of Madeira near Pacific Grove, California, LEFT.

tinus), its cousin the Korean spicebush (*V. carlesii*), and the late summer flowers of Sweet pepperbush, colors are pale yellow, pink, blue, and lavender, with a bit of sparkling white. A pink penstemon holds the attention of hummingbirds, while a late-summer-blooming *Clematis viticella* hybrid makes the viburnums do double-duty.

Just steps away from the kitchen, between the patio and the lawn, is a swath of herbs — among the favorite plants of butterflies — planted for ornament as well as their usefulness. The

The scent of this bee balm,
ABOVE, *attracts butterflies. Asters,* BELOW,
bloom in the fall.

Butterflies are among the most engaging creatures on earth. Some butterfly devotees are especially fascinated by the dramatic transformation they undergo during their life cycle. Others are intrigued by their mysterious habits. Whatever your fancy, butterflies are wonderful candidates for your appreciation. As you observe butterflies in your garden, you may wish to ponder the great lengths to which "mad" collectors of bygone centuries went simply to glimpse them. Much of the wilderness they combed has disappeared, so take pride in your efforts to ensure the butterfly's survival.

purple foliage of sedum and sage blends beautifully with the gray of pussytoes (*Antennaria* spp.), lavender, and woolly and silver thymes, and with the blue of rue and tussocky evergreen oats. Golden sage and marjoram, and white-splashed variegated marjoram complete the foliar collage. Wands of 'Hopley's Purple' oregano, pink lollipops of chives, and the similar nonstop flowers of sea pink (*Armeria* spp.) augment this tapestry of color and texture, which is as tasteful as it is tasty, both to you and your butterflies.

APPENDICES

Plants by Mail

ANDRE VIETTE FARM AND NURSERY
RT. 1, BOX 16
FISHERSVILLE, VA 22939
UNUSUAL PERENNIALS, DAYLILIES, HOSTAS,
IRISES, AND SHRUBS.
CATALOG AVAILABLE.

BLUESTONE PERENNIALS
7211 MIDDLE RIDGE RD.
MADISON, OH 44057
WIDE SELECTION OF STANDARD PERENNIALS.
PLANTS ARE SMALL, BUT INEXPENSIVE; YOUR
PATIENCE AND SKILL CAN SAVE YOU MONEY.

CANYON CREEK NURSERY
3527 DRY CREEK RD.
OROVILLE, CA 95965
THE BEST CULTIVARS OF PERENNIALS,
WELL DESCRIBED AND WELL SHIPPED.
GOOD CATALOG AVAILABLE.

CAPRICE FARM NURSERY
15425 SW PLEASANT HILL RD.
SHERWOOD, OR 97140
PEONIES, TREE PEONIES, DAYLILIES, AND
JAPANESE IRISES. CATALOG AVAILABLE.

FORESTFARM
990 TETHEROW RD.
WILLIAMS, OR 97544-9599
HUGE, MOUTH-WATERING LIST OF
PERENNIALS AND WOODY PLANTS.
A MUST. CATALOG AVAILABLE.

K. VAN BOURGONDIEN AND SONS, INC.
245 FARMINGDALE RD.
BABYLON, NY 11702
DUTCH-RAISED BULBS AND PERENNIALS,
SOME QUITE UNUSUAL.

KURT BLUEMEL, INC.
2740 GREENE LN.
BALDWIN, MD 21023
THE DEFINITIVE LIST OF ORNAMENTAL
GRASSES. CATALOG AVAILABLE.

LAMB NURSERIES
E. 101 SHARP AVE.
SPOKANE, WA 99202
ONE OF THE BEST LISTS OF PERENNIALS,
WITH A FEW SHRUBS.

McCLURE AND ZIMMERMAN
108 W. WINNEBAGO
BOX 368
FRIESLAND, WI 53935
BULBS ONLY; SOME VERY UNUSUAL
AND DESIRABLE.

MONTROSE NURSERY
P.O. BOX 957
HILLSBORO, NC 27278
MANY OUT-OF-THE-ORDINARY PERENNIALS,
SOME NATIVE, DESCRIBED IN GREAT DETAIL.
CATALOG AVAILABLE.

PARK SEED CO.
COKESBURY RD.
GREENWOOD, SC 29649-0001
ONE OF THE MOST HIGHLY
RESPECTED SEED FIRMS.

PICKERING NURSERIES, INC.
670 KINGSTON RD.

PICKERING, ON, CANADA L1V 1A6
ROSES, ROSES, AND MORE ROSES.
ALL KINDS AND CLASSES, INCLUDING SPECIES
AND DAVID AUSTIN ENGLISH ROSES.
BARGAIN PRICES, TOO. CATALOG AVAILABLE.

PLANTS OF THE SOUTHWEST
930 BACA ST.
SANTA FE, NM 87501
PLANTS NATIVE TO (OR ADAPTED TO) THE
TOUGH CONDITIONS OF THE SOUTHWEST AND
GREAT BASIN. FROM PRAIRIE GRASSES
SUITABLE FOR LAWNS, THROUGH WILDFLOWERS,
PERENNIALS, AND SHRUBS. PLANTS AND SEEDS.

ROSES BY FRED EDMUNDS, INC.
6235 SW KAHLE RD.
WILSONVILLE, OR 97070
MODERN BEDDING ROSES, WITH HONEST
INFORMATION AND EVALUATIONS.

STOKES SEEDS, INC.
BOX 548
BUFFALO, NY 14240
GOOD SELECTION OF FLOWERS,
AS WELL AS VEGETABLES.

W. ATLEE BURPEE AND CO.
WARMINSTER, PA 18974
SOME PLANTS, BUT PRIMARILY
A SEED CATALOG.

WAYSIDE GARDENS CO.
HODGES, SC 29695
COLLECTION OF FINE BUT PRICEY PLANTS.
LAVISHLY ILLUSTRATED CATALOG AVAILABLE.

WHITE FLOWER FARM
LITCHFIELD, CT 06759
THIS CATALOG READS LIKE A MINI
ENCYCLOPEDIA. GOOD LISTING OF STANDARD
SORTS OF PLANTS. CATALOG AVAILABLE.

WOODLANDERS, INC.
1128 COLLETON AVE.
AIKEN, SC 29801
WONDERFUL OFFERING OF NATIVE AND
EXOTIC TREES, SHRUBS, VINES, PERENNIALS,
FERNS, ETC. SOME OF OUR MOST ORNAMEN-
TAL NATIVES COME FROM THE SOUTHEAST,
AND THIS IS WHERE TO BUY THEM.

Butterfly Gardens to Visit

BUTTERFLY WORLD
TRADEWINDS PARK SOUTH
3600 W. SAMPLE RD.
COCONUT CREEK, FL 33063
(305) 977-4400
TROPICAL BUTTERFLY HOUSE,
OUTDOOR BUTTERFLY GARDEN.

BUTTERFLY WORLD AT MARINE WORLD,
AFRICA USA
MARINE WORLD PARKWAY
VALLEJO, CA 94589
(707) 644-4000
TROPICAL BUTTERFLY HOUSE.

CECIL B. DAY BUTTERFLY CENTER
CALLAWAY GARDENS
PINE MOUNTAIN, GA 31822
(404) 663-2281
TROPICAL BUTTERFLY HOUSE,
OUTDOOR BUTTERFLY GARDEN.

CINCINNATI ZOO
3400 VINE ST.
CINCINNATI, OH 45220
(513) 281-4701
TROPICAL BUTTERFLY HOUSE,
SMALL OUTDOOR GARDEN.

DES MOINES BOTANICAL GARDENS
909 E. RIVER DR.
DES MOINES, IA 50316
(515) 283-4148
TROPICAL BUTTERFLY HOUSE.

VANCOUVER ISLAND BUTTERFLY WORLD
341 W. CRESCENT RD.
QUALICUM BEACH, BC, CANADA V0R 2T0
(604) 752-9319
BUTTERFLY HOUSE.

Butterfly Organizations

Entomological Society of America
4603 Calvert Rd.
College Park, MD 20740
Covers all insects, not just butterflies.

The Lepidoptera Research Foundation
Santa Barbara Museum
of Natural History
2559 Puesta del Sol Rd.
Santa Barbara, CA 93105
Publishes a journal of research
relating to butterflies and moths.

The *Xerces* Society
International Organization for
Invertebrate Habitat Conservation
10 SW Ash St.
Portland, OR 97204
A perhaps less academic and more
practical organization for involvement
in butterfly-related topics.
Sort of a Sierra Club for butterflies.

Young Entomologists' Society
Dept. of Entomology
Michigan State University
E. Lansing, MI 48824
Puts out a quarterly bulletin
with young people in mind.

Native-Plant Organizations

New England Wild Flower Society
Garden in the Woods
Hemenway Rd.
Framingham, MA 01701
For $1.00, they'll send you a listing of
native-plant societies for most states.

Further Reading

BUTTERFLIES

BORROR, DONALD J., AND RICHARD E. WHITE. *A Field Guide to the Insects of America North of Mexico.* BOSTON: HOUGHTON MIFFLIN, 1970.

BREWER, JO. *Wings in the Meadow.* NEW YORK: HOUGHTON MIFFLIN, 1967.

BROWER, LINCOLN P. "Monarch Migration." *Natural History,* JUNE/JULY 1977.

EMMEL, THOMAS C. *Butterflies: Their World, Their Life Cycle, Their Behavior.* NEW YORK: ALFRED A. KNOPF, 1975.

KLOTS, ALEXANDER B. *A Field Guide to the Butterflies of North America East of the Great Plains.* BOSTON: HOUGHTON MIFFLIN, 1951.

ORDISH, GEORGE. *The Year of the Butterfly.* NEW YORK: CHARLES SCRIBNER'S SONS, 1975.

PARENTI, UMBERTO. *The World of Butterflies and Moths.* NEW YORK: G. P. PUTNAM'S SONS, 1978.

PETERSON, ROGER TORY, ROBERT MICHAEL PYLE, AND SARAH ANN HUGHES. *A Field Guide to Butterflies Coloring Book.* BOSTON: HOUGHTON MIFFLIN, 1983.

PYLE, ROBERT MICHAEL. *The Audubon Society Field Guide to North American Butterflies.* NEW YORK: ALFRED A. KNOPF, 1981.

SCOTT, JAMES A. *The Butterflies of North America.* STANFORD, CALIF.: STANFORD UNIVERSITY PRESS, 1986.

SMART, PAUL. *The Illustrated Encyclopedia of the Butterfly World.* NEW YORK: CHARTWELL BOOKS, 1984.

TYLER, HAMILTON A. *The Swallowtail Butterflies of North America.* HEALDSBURG, CALIF.: NATUREGRAPH PUBLISHERS, 1975.

URQUHART, F. A. *The Monarch Butterfly.* TORONTO: UNIVERSITY OF TORONTO PRESS, 1960.

WATSON, ALLAN, AND PAUL E. S. WHALLEY. *The Dictionary of Butterflies and Moths in Color.* NEW YORK: SIMON AND SCHUSTER, 1983.

BUTTERFLY GARDENING

DAMROSCH, BARBARA. *Theme Gardens.* NEW YORK: WORKMAN PUB. CO., 1982.

TEKULSKY, MATHEW. *The Butterfly Garden.* HARVARD AND BOSTON: HARVARD COMMON PRESS, 1985.

IN ADDITION, THE *Xerces* SOCIETY (SEE UNDER BUTTERFLY ORGANIZATIONS) PUBLISHES MANY INFORMATIVE LEAFLETS.

GENERAL GARDENING

BECKETT, KENNETH A. *CLIMBING PLANTS.* PORTLAND, OREG.: TIMBER PRESS, 1983.

BRUCE, HAL. *HOW TO GROW WILDFLOWERS AND WILD SHRUBS AND TREES IN YOUR OWN GARDEN.* NEW YORK: ALFRED A. KNOPF, 1976.

CHAMBERLIN, SUSAN. *HEDGES, SCREENS, AND ESPALIERS.* TUCSON: HP BOOKS, 1983.

CHATTO, BETH. *THE GREEN TAPESTRY.* NEW YORK: SIMON AND SCHUSTER, 1989.

DUFFIELD, MARY ROSE, AND WARREN D. JONES. *PLANTS FOR DRY CLIMATES.* LOS ANGELES: HP BOOKS, N.D.

HEADSTROM, RICHARD. *SUBURBAN WILD FLOWERS: AN INTRODUCTION TO THE COMMON WILDFLOWERS OF YOUR BACK YARD AND LOCAL PARK.* ENGLEWOOD CLIFFS, N.J.: PRENTICE-HALL, 1984.

HOBHOUSE, PENELOPE. *COLOR IN YOUR GARDEN.* BOSTON: LITTLE, BROWN, AND CO., 1985.

JOHNSON, HUGH. *THE PRINCIPLES OF GARDENING.* NEW YORK: SIMON AND SCHUSTER, 1979.

LOVEJOY, ANN. *THE YEAR IN BLOOM.* SEATTLE: SASQUATCH BOOKS, 1987.

PHILLIPS, ROGER, AND MARTIN RIX. *ROSES.* NEW YORK: RANDOM HOUSE, 1988.

PHILLIPS, ROGER, AND MARTIN RIX. *SHRUBS.* NEW YORK: RANDOM HOUSE, 1989.

SPERKA, MARIE. *GROWING WILDFLOWERS: A GARDENER'S GUIDE.* NEW YORK: CHARLES SCRIBNER'S SONS, 1974.

STEFFEK, EDWIN F. *THE NEW WILD FLOWERS AND HOW TO GROW THEM.* BEAVERTON, OREG.: TIMBER PRESS, 1983.

SUNSET BOOKS. *SUNSET NEW WESTERN GARDEN BOOK.* MENLO PARK, CALIF.: LANE PUBLISHING, 1989.

THOMAS, GRAHAM STUART. *THE ART OF PLANTING.* BOSTON, DAVID R. GODINE, 1984.

THOMAS, GRAHAM STUART. *PERENNIAL GARDEN PLANTS.* NEW YORK: DAVID MCKAY CO., INC., 1976.

WRIGHT, MICHAEL. *COMPLETE HANDBOOK OF GARDEN PLANTS.* NEW YORK: FACTS ON FILE, 1984.

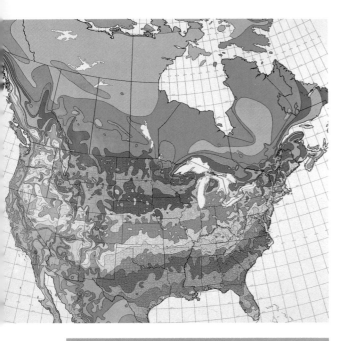

USDA Plant Hardiness Zone Map

Photo courtesy of the
Agricultural Research Service, USDA

AVERAGE ANNUAL MINIMUM TEMPERATURE

Temperature (°C)	Zone	Temperature (°F)
−45.6 and below	1	below −50
−42.8 to −45.5	2a	−45 to −50
−40.0 to −42.7	2b	−40 to −45
−37.3 to −40.0	3a	−35 to −40
−34.5 to −37.2	3b	−30 to −35
−31.7 to −34.4	4a	−25 to −30
−28.9 to −31.6	4b	−20 to −25
−26.2 to −28.8	5a	−15 to −20
−23.4 to −26.1	5b	−10 to −15
−20.6 to −23.3	6a	−5 to −10
−17.8 to −20.5	6b	0 to −5
−15.0 to −17.7	7a	5 to 0
−12.3 to −15.0	7b	10 to 5
−9.5 to −12.2	8a	15 to 10
−6.7 to −9.4	8b	20 to 15
−3.9 to −6.6	9a	25 to 20
−1.2 to −3.8	9b	30 to 25
1.6 to −1.1	10a	35 to 30
4.4 to 1.7	10b	40 to 35
4.5 and above	11	40 and above

Photo Credits

Gene Ahrens, 80–1, 86
Frederick D. Atwood, 31 bottom, 104, 107
© Liz Ball, 108, 136
© Philip Beaurline/Photo/Nats, 88
© Gay Bumgarner/Photo/Nats, 18, 31 top, 54, 64–5, 120
© Thomas C. Boyden, 19, 25, 27, 30, 47, 48, 49, 51, 57, 59, 60–1, 77, 78, 79, 109, 110, 111 bottom, 113, 134–5
© Priscilla Connell/Photo/Nats, 41, 50, 68, 69

© Molly Dean, 2, 14–15, 20, 125 right
© Kerry T. Givens, 53, 73
Robert Kourik, 134
Dorothy S. Long/Photo/Nats, 35
John A. Lynch/Photo/Nats, 10
© Robert E. Lyons/Photo/Nats, 89, 90–1, 95
© Jeff March/Photo/Nats, 12, 63, 111 top
© Margarette Mead, 13, 17, 122

Gary Meszaros, 24, 36–7, 42, 44–5, 52, 55, 70, 74–5, 101
Paul E. Meyers, 34, 56, 61, 67, 72–3
Joanne Pavia, 114
© Lanny Provo, 125 left
© Ann Reilly/Photo/Nats, 92, 94
© J. H. Robinson, 58–9
© Gary Vestal, 28–9, 66, 70–1
© Muriel Williams/Photo/Nats, 32 (2), 33 (2), 76
© Alice Yarborough, 6–7, 83, 84, 97, 99, 116, 118–19, 135

INDEX

Page numbers of illustrations are italicized